WebPlus X8
Resource Guide

Contacting Serif

Help with your Product

ComʈlunityPlus   community.serif.com
Get answers and ask questions in the Serif community!

Additional Serif information

Serif website   www.serif.com

Main office

Address   The Software Centre, PO Box 2000
Nottingham, NG11 7GW, UK

Phone   (0115) 914 2000

Phone (Registration) (0800) 376 1989
+44 800 376 1989
800-794-6876 (US, Canada)

Phone (Sales)   (0800) 376 7070
+44 800 376 7070
800-489-6703 (US, Canada)

Customer Service   0845 345 6770
800-489-6720 (US, Canada)

Fax   (0115) 914 2020

Credits

This Resource Guide, and the software described in it, is furnished under an end user License Agreement, which is included with the product. The agreement specifies the permitted and prohibited uses.

Trademarks

Serif is a registered trademark of Serif (Europe) Ltd.

WebPlus is a registered trademark of Serif (Europe) Ltd.

All Serif product names are trademarks of Serif (Europe) Ltd.

Microsoft, Windows, and the Windows logo are registered trademarks of Microsoft Corporation. All other trademarks acknowledged.

Windows Vista and the Windows Vista Start button are trademarks or registered trademarks of Microsoft Corporation in the United States and/or other countries.

Google+ social service, Google Maps, Google Analytics web analytics service, and Google AdSense advertising service are trademarks of Google Inc.

Copyrights

Digital Images ©2008 Hemera Technologies Inc. All Rights Reserved.

Portions images ©1997-2002 Nova Development Corporation; ©1995 Expressions Computer Software; ©1996-98 CreatiCom, Inc.; ©1996 Cliptoart; ©1997 Multimedia Agency Corporation; ©1997-98 Seattle Support Group. Rights of all parties reserved.

This application was developed using LEADTOOLS, copyright © 1991-2007 LEAD Technologies, Inc. ALL Rights Reserved.

THE PROXIMITY HYPHENATION SYSTEM © 1989 Proximity Technology Inc. All rights reserved.

THE PROXIMITY/COLLINS DATABASE® © 1990 William Collins Sons & Co. Ltd.; © 1990 Proximity Technology Inc. All rights reserved.

THE PROXIMITY/MERRIAM-WEBSTER DATABASE® © 1990 Merriam-Webster Inc.; © 1990 Proximity Technology Inc. All rights reserved.

The Sentry Spelling-Checker Engine © 2000 Wintertree Software Inc.

The ThesDB Thesaurus Engine © 1993-97 Wintertree Software Inc.

WGrammar Grammar-Checker Engine © 1998 Wintertree Software Inc.

Andrei Stcherbatchenko, Ferdinand Prantl

PayPal © 1999-2012 PayPal. All rights reserved.

Introduction

Welcome to the WebPlus X8 Resource Guide.

This Resource Guide covers the best techniques for using the fundamental tools in WebPlus, from beginner- to advanced-level, and provides creative inspiration for producing a website.

1: Tutorials

This chapter will help you work with the tools and content available in WebPlus X8. You'll learn how to use these fundamental tools and professional features to create a dynamic and eye-catching website. Each tutorial contains a wealth of information and techniques for using WebPlus.

2: Creative Showcase

We showcase a few Pro Design Template and theme layout sites which you can use to get started easily. Instructions on accessing these templates and theme layouts are also included.

Working with tutorials

Throughout the Resource Guide, you'll be prompted to access resource files from the **Startup Assistant** and **Assets** tab within WebPlus. These files have been provided to get you started or to help focus on a key learning point. Details for accessing these files are provided within the tutorial.

We recommend working through the tutorials in sequence.

Useful icons

Here is a quick guide to the icons you'll find useful along the way.

 We'll remind you save your work with these helpful save points.

 These give you an estimate of how long a tutorial will take to complete.

 For guidance, tutorials are graded between 1 (beginner) - 3 (advanced).

 This is a note. Notes provide useful information about the program or a particular technique.

 This is a tip. Our tips provide information that will help you with your projects.

 This is a warning! We don't want to make you panic but when you see this icon, you need to pay attention to the steps as they will be particularly important.

Exploring WebPlus X8

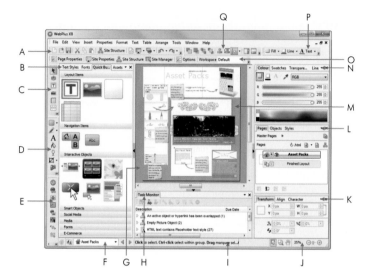

(A) Standard toolbar, (B) Text Styles, Fonts, Quick Build, and Assets tabs, (C) Basic toolbar, (D) Drawing toolbar, (E) Properties toolbar, (F) Page Locator, (G) Pasteboard area, (H) Task Monitor tab, (I) Hintline toolbar, (J) View options, (K) Transform, Align, and Character tabs, (L) Pages, Objects, and Styles tabs, (M) Page area, (N) Colour, Swatches, Transparency, and Line tabs, (O) Context toolbar, (P) Colour toolbar, (Q) Arrange toolbar.

The WebPlus workspace

- Horizontal and vertical **toolbars** and **tabs**, used to access WebPlus commands and tools.

- Move the mouse pointer around the screen and you'll see pop-up **tooltips** that identify toolbar buttons and flyouts.

- Right-click any object or page region to bring up a **context menu** of functions.

Table of Contents

Tutorials

1

Setting up a new site

30 min

Creating a website in WebPlus doesn't need to be a complicated affair. Even if you want to start from scratch, the process is a relatively simple one. In this tutorial, we'll show you how to set up your site ready to add site content.

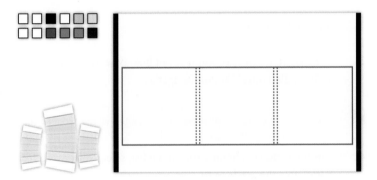

By the end of this tutorial you will be able to:

- Customize the initial setup of your website.

- Add new pages.

- Preview your site in a browser.

- Add a Favourites icon (Favicon).

- Set up margin guides.

Whether you are creating a website for a business, charity, or club, or setting up a personal website, it is worth researching potential web addresses before starting your design. Your web address (URL) should be easy to remember and should have a strong link to your site name. Also consider acquiring social media profiles which are identical (or close to) your URL.

Let's begin...

1. From the **File** menu, click **Startup Assistant**.

2. On the left, click **New Site**.

3. On the right, in the **Site Name** input box, type the name of your site. We called ours "Million Budget".

By naming your site here, it will populate throughout your site and provide instant branding on every page.

4. From the **Colour Scheme** drop-down list, select your preferred scheme. We chose **Clean 01**.

Your setup should now resemble ours...

5. Leave the remaining settings set to the default and click **Start new site**.

The Site Name specified in step 3 appears as the default File name in the **Save As** dialog.

6. Navigate to your chosen location and click **Save**.

Your new site opens with the Home page displayed in the workspace. We'll add some additional pages to begin building our site.

Adding pages

All websites contain a Home page (for details, see the *Sliders and text* tutorial on p. 63) to greet visitors. Any other pages are optional, though we highly recommend adding a page which allows visitors to easily get in touch with you.

To add a new page:

1. On the **Pages** tab, click the down arrow on the 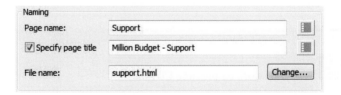 **Add new page or link** button and select **New Blank Page**.

2. In the **Page Properties** dialog:

Naming		
Page name:	Support	
☑ Specify page title	Million Budget - Support	
File name:	support.html	Change...

- In the **Page name** input box, drag to select the default name and then type 'Support'. This is used for navigation purposes.

- Select the **Specify page title** option and update the contents of the adjacent input box.

The page title has already been pre-populating using the Site Name you specified when you create your site from the Startup Assistant.

- In the **File name** input box, drag to select the default name and then type 'support.html'.

We recommend that all HTML names remain in lower case and do not contain spaces.

- Click **OK**.

The new page is added to your site and displayed in the workspace.

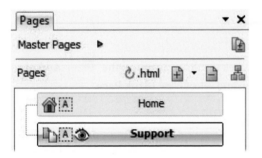

The navigation bar also updates to display this newly added page.

Save your work by pressing **Ctrl+S.**

Previewing your site

Previewing your site in a browser window gives you a great indication of what the final published website will look like.

> We recommend testing compatibility for a range of browsers such as Internet Explorer, Firefox, Chrome, Safari, and Opera.

To preview your site in a browser:

- On the **Standard** toolbar, click the down arrow on the **Preview site** button and select **Preview in {browser of choice}**.

> If you leave the browser open with your site displayed, changes to your site can be quickly viewed by refreshing/reloading the page directly in the browser (commonly by pressing **F5**).

If we examine the displayed information, you'll get an idea of how visitors to your website will see the settings you've implemented.

The page title of the current page is displayed on the tab and the file name is displayed in the address bar. If a page from your website is added to a visitor's bookmarks, the page title is used to identify it by default. (We added our Home page to our browser's favourites bar.)

Page titles are also important as they identify the contents of website pages to search engines.

Adding a Favourites Icon

Adding a Favourites icon (Favicon) gives your site a graphic identity and credibility, and helps it to stand out in a cluttered list of bookmarks or favourites.

To add a favicon:

1. On the context toolbar, click ⊞ **Site Properties**.

2. In the **Site Properties** dialog:

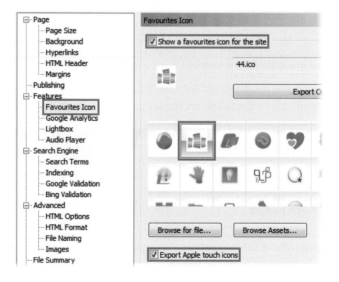

- On the left, from the **Features** category, select the **Favourites Icon** sub-category.

- Select the **Show a favourites icon for the site** option.

- Select an asset from the gallery.

- Select the **Export Apple touch icons** option.

- Click **OK**.

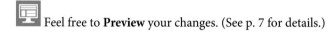 Feel free to **Preview** your changes. (See p. 7 for details.)

Depending on the browser, the Favicon is displayed in the tab next to the page name and/or before a website's URL in a browser's address bar. The icon also displays next to the website's name in a list of bookmarks, when a visitor bookmarks your site or adds it to their 'favourites'.

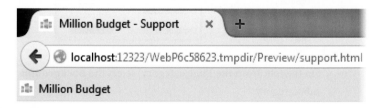

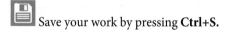 Save your work by pressing **Ctrl+S**.

Setting the site background

When previewing the site, you may have noticed there was no clear distinction between the site background and the site page. This is because, by default, the site background is set to scheme colour 1 and the page colour to transparent. This may suit your needs, but we'll show you how you can update the settings to define the page against the background.

To adjust background settings:

1. On the context toolbar, click 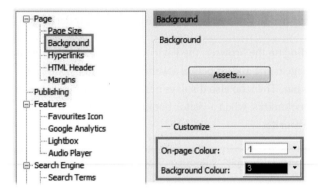 **Site Properties**.

2. In the **Site Properties** dialog:

- On the left, from the **Page** category, select the **Background** sub-category.

- From the **On-page Colour** drop-down list, select **Scheme Colour 1**.

- From the **Background Colour** drop-down list, select **Scheme Colour 3**. The **Preview** on the right updates as you make your changes.

> This scheme colour combination works well for our currently selected scheme. Depending on the scheme you chose, you may need to select alternative contrasting scheme colours

- Click **OK**.

Save your work by pressing **Ctrl+S.**

 Feel free to **Preview** your changes. (See p. 7 for details.)

Setting up margins

Before we begin putting our design together, it is worth thinking about the general layout of our site pages.

To help visitors navigate around and find information easily, we're going to ensure page elements appear in the same place on each page. We will also design our site using a header and footer, and use measurements which are compatible with sites which can be viewed on mobile devices.

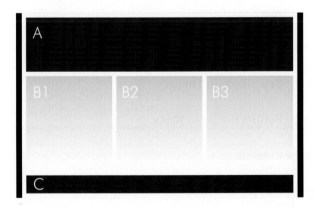

A - Header measuring 930 x 180 pix, B - Page elements measuring 300 pix wide (height variable), C - Footer measuring 930 x 60 pix. All gaps measure 15 pix.

To achieve this consistent layout we'll set up margins.

To set up margins:

1. On the context toolbar, click 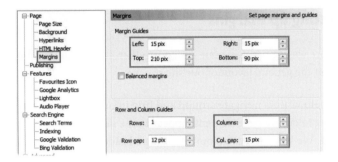 **Site Properties**.

2. In the **Site Properties** dialog:

- On the left, from the **Page** category, select the **Margins** sub-category.

- Set the **Left** and **Right** margins to **15 pix**.

- Set the **Top** margin to **210 pix**.

- Set the **Bottom** margin to **90 pix**.

- Set the **Columns** to **3**.

- Set the **Col. gap** to **15 pix**.

- Click **OK**.

The setting will ensure margin guides appear consistently on all pages, regardless of their width or height.

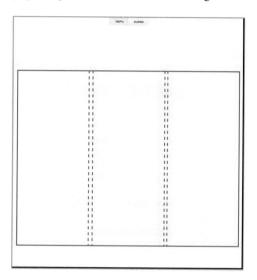

When laying out page content, working within these guides will help visitors find information quickly. To ensure we do not accidently move our guides, we'll lock them.

 Save your work by pressing **Ctrl+S.**

To lock guides:

1. On the context toolbar, click 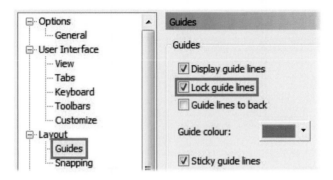 **Options**.

2. In the **Options** dialog:

- On the left, from the **Layout** category, select the **Guides** sub-category.

- Select the **Lock guide lines** option.

- Click **OK**.

That's it! Your site is now set up ready for you to add content. The next recommended step is to add content to a Master page.

> You may wish to review your site development progress by checking the **Program Hints** section of the **Task Monitor** tab. Select any suggested processes you have completed and click **Mark as Fixed** to cross them off the list.

Master pages and Text Styles

 30 min

Master pages allow you to share an underlying design across multiple site pages. This allows you to achieve consistency throughout your site, and save yourself a lot of time and effort in the process!

By the end of this tutorial you will be able to:

● Access a Master page.

● Create a header and footer using panels.

● Add a logo and site information, such as the site name.

● Update text styles.

● Add copyright information.

> If you have already completed the *Setting up a new site* tutorial on p. 3, you can use your saved project as the starting point for this tutorial.

Let's begin...

1. From the **File** menu, click **Startup Assistant**.

2. On the left, click **Open**.

3. From the gallery on the right, select **WPX8 Tutorial 01.wpp**.

WPX8 Tutorial 01.wpp

If the tutorial file is not available from the gallery, click **Sample files**.

From the **Open** dialog, select the file, select **Open as untitled**, and click **Open**.

Alternatively, in the **Open** dialog, navigate to the folder where you saved your project file from the *Setting up a new site* tutorial on p. 3, select it and click **Open**.

A site will open in the workspace with two pages and page guides.

Why use Master pages?

Master pages are like transparent sheets behind or in front of your main site pages.

When you add text frames, pictures, or other elements to the Master page, they appear in the same position on all site pages that use that Master page.

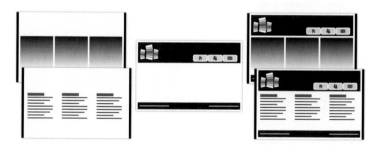

What you place on a Master page is entirely up to you and often depends on the type of site you are creating. Typical elements that you'd place on a Master page include:

- navigation elements (see the *Navigation bars and Sitemaps* tutorial on p. 39 for more details).

- company name, logo and/or contact details.

Master pages simplify site maintenance as objects placed on a Master page only need updating once.

So let's access the Master page in our site and begin designing!

To access the master page:

1. On the **Pages** tab, click **Master Pages**.

2. Double-click the **Master A** thumbnail.

The Master page is displayed in the workspace.

We'll begin our design using panels to create a page header and footer.

Creating a header and footer using panels

Headers and footers are a great way of organizing information and navigation on a website. We'll create these using panels. Panels can host a whole range of content including text, pictures, navigation bars, and maps. Once content has been placed on a panel, it becomes attached to that panel. Moving the panel will also move all the content on it.

To add a panel:

1. On the **Quick Build** tab, in the **Layout Items** category, drag the **Panel** layout item to the page.

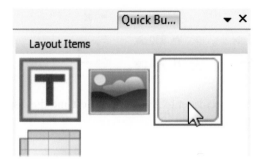

2. In the **Insert Panel** dialog, click **OK**.

3. On the **Swatches** tab, select **Scheme Colour 3**.

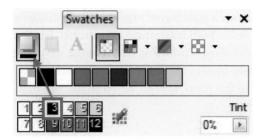

The scheme colour is applied to the panel's fill.

4. With the panel still selected, on the **Transform** tab:

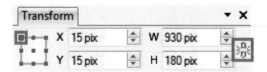

- Ensure the object is set to **Anchor Top Left** and the **Aspect Ratio** is **Unlocked**.

- Set **X** to **15 pix** and **Y** to **15 pix**.

- Set **W** (Width) to **930 pix** and **H** (Height) to **180 pix**.

The panel is resized and positioned on the page precisely. The measurements meet the criteria we set in the *Setting up a new site* tutorial on p. 11.

We'll duplicate this panel to create a footer.

To duplicate an object:

1. Hold down the **Ctrl** key and then drag the panel.

2. Release the **Ctrl** key and mouse button.

A copy of the panel is created.

3. With the panel still selected, on the **Transform** tab:

- Ensure the object is set to **Anchor Top Left** and the **Aspect Ratio** is **Unlocked**.

- Set **X** to **15 pix** and **Y** to **925 pix**.

- Set **H** (Height) to **60 pix**.

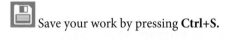Save your work by pressing **Ctrl+S.**

Our basic Master page layout, with header and footer, is now
complete.

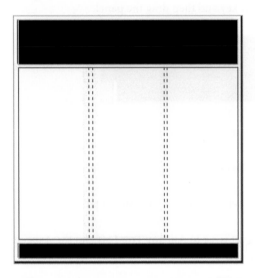

 It closely resembles the layout we originally sketched out in the *Setting up a new site* tutorial on p. 11.

However, to ensure our footer always appears at the bottom of the
page, we need to attach it there.

To attach an object to the bottom of the page:

* With the footer panel still selected, from the **Arrange** menu,
  select **Attach to Bottom of Page**.

The footer panel will now move in relation to the bottom of the page
if a page is resized.

 Feel free to **Preview** your changes. (See p. 7 for details.)

Adding content to the header

Now we have our basic page structure in place, let's begin adding elements to our site. We'll focus on the header and the objects which appear on them, such as a company logo and site name.

To add a logo:

1. On the **Assets** tab, click ▢ **Browse** to open the **Asset Browser**.

2. On the left, in the **Pack Files** section, click to select the **Logos** pack. The logos from all installed packs are displayed in the main pane.

3. In the main pane, click a logo of your choice.

The green ✅ shows that the asset has been added to the tab. The ▦ icon indicates the object is schemed.

4. Click **Close**.

5.   On the **Assets** tab, the **Graphics** category should be displayed (if not, click the header).

6.   Drag the logo to the pasteboard.

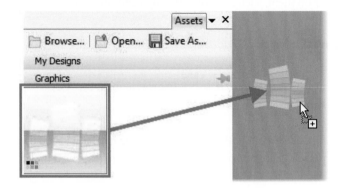

7.   With the logo still selected, drag the object's  move button to position it neatly on the header panel.

Next we'll add our site name...

To add the site name:

1. On the **Drawing** toolbar, click $\textbf{A}$ **Insert Artistic Text**.

2. Click on the header panel to the right of the logo.

3. On the context toolbar, from the **Style** drop-down list, select **Heading 1**.

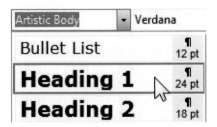

4. From the **Text** menu, select **Insert>Information>Site Info**.

5. In the **Site Information** dialog, select **Site Name** and click **OK**.

The site name is added to the header panel.

However, the text is difficult to read as the Text Styles do not currently complement the colour scheme we have in place. We'll look at updating this next, before we add content to our footer.

You can change the name of your site (and other information) from the **File Summary** category in the **Site Properties** dialog (accessible from the **Properties** menu).

 Save your work by pressing **Ctrl+S.**

Updating text styles

A text style is a set of character and/or paragraph attributes saved as a group. When you apply a style to text, you apply the whole group of attributes in just one step. We'll update the preset styles to suit our needs, but before we do, let's quickly discuss fonts.

All available fonts on your computer are displayed in the **Fonts** tab. These are divided into categories by default. **Websafe** fonts are available on all computers and designing with these fonts will guarantee your website looks identical on all viewing platforms. **Embeddable** fonts give you more creative freedom. These fonts will be embedded with your website so that even if a font is not installed on a visitor's computer, they will be able to view text as you have designed it. See *Using fonts* in WebPlus Help for more information on fonts.

To speed up your design process, you can add any fonts to a customizable **Favourites** category.

To add fonts to the Favourites category:

- On the **Fonts** tab:

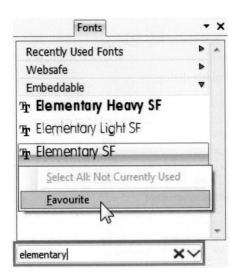

- In the search box at the bottom, type 'elementary'.

- In the **Embeddable** category, right-click **Elementary SF** and select **Favourite**.

- Repeat the above steps to add **Elementary Heavy SF** to the **Favourites** category.

Now, onto updating our text styles...

To update the base style:

1. On the **Text Styles** tab, select 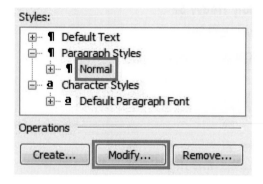 **Manage**.

2. In the **Text Style Palette** dialog:

- From the **Paragraph Styles** category, select **Normal**.

- Click **Modify**.

3. In the **Text Style** dialog:

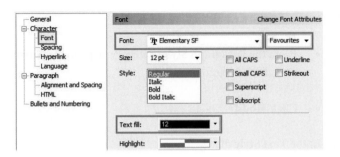

- From the **Character** category, select the **Font** sub-category.

- From the second **Font** drop-down list (displays **Websafe** by default), select **Favourites**.

- From the first **Font** drop-down list, select **Elementary SF**.

- From the **Text fill** drop-down list, select **Scheme Colour 12**.

- Click **OK**.

Modifying the Normal style will affect all other styles which are based on it (such as Body). We'll also update the generic Headings style.

To update a parent style:

1. In the **Text Style Palette** dialog:

   - From the **Paragraph Styles** category, expand the **Normal** branch, and select **Headings**.

   - Click **Modify**.

2. In the **Text Style** dialog:

   - From the **Character** category, select the **Font** sub-category.

   - From the second **Font** drop-down list (displays **Websafe** by default), select **Favourites**.

   - From the first **Font** drop-down list, select **Elementary Heavy SF**.

   - Click **OK**.

The changes made to the Headings parent style is adopted by all the child styles underneath.

Currently our text set to Heading 1 appears on a dark background, so let's modify our Heading 1 style to adopt a light colour.

To update an individual style:

I. In the **Text Style Palette** dialog:

- From the **Paragraph Styles** category, expand the **Headings** branch, and select **Heading 1**.

- Click **Modify**.

2. In the **Text Style** dialog:

- From the **Character** category, select the **Font** sub-category.

- Select the **All CAPS** option.

- From the **Text fill** drop-down list, select **Scheme Colour 1**.

- Click **OK**.

3. Back in the **Text Style Palette** dialog, click **Close**.

The styles in the Text Styles tab and the text on the page update to reflect your changes.

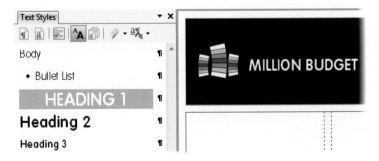

Adding context-sensitive text

You can place text on the page which is context-sensitive and will update depending on which page is being viewed on the site. We'll show you this by adding the page name under the site's header.

To add context-sensitive text:

1. On the **Quick Build** tab, in the **Layout Items** category, click the **Text Frame** layout item.

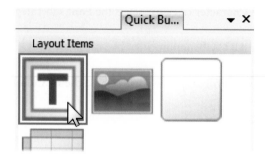

2. Click anywhere on the page.

3. On the context toolbar, from the **Style** drop-down list, select **Heading 2**.

4. From the **Text** menu, select **Insert>Information>Page Info**.

5. In the **Web Page Information** dialog, select **Page Name** and click **OK**.

6. On the **Transform** tab:

- Ensure the object is set to **Anchor Top Left** and the **Aspect Ratio** is **Unlocked**.

- Set **X** to **15 pix** and **Y** to **210 pix**.

- Set **W** (Width) to **300 pix** and **H** (Height) to **35 pix**.

The text will now update depending on the page viewed. The page's name will be displayed.

Let's finish our Master page design by adding a copyright to the footer.

 Save your work by pressing **Ctrl+S.**

 Feel free to **Preview** your changes. (See p. 7 for details.)

Adding copyright to a footer

By adding copyright text to the footer of your website, it immediately identifies the author and establishes the copyright of content on the site. By adding this information to a Master page, it will display on all pages in your site.

To add copyright text:

1. On the **Quick Build** tab, in the **Layout Items** category, click the **Text Frame** layout item.

2. Click on the right side of the footer panel.

3. On the **Text Styles** tab:

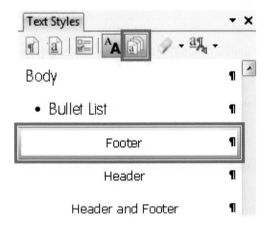

- Click **Show All** to display all available text styles.

- Select **Footer**.

4. To insert a copyright symbol, click on the **Text** menu and then click **Insert>Symbol>Copyright**.

5. Next press the Spacebar and type your name and the year.

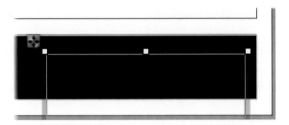

The current Footer text style isn't very readable. Let's modify this to suit our design. As the Footer style is based on the Header and Footer parent style, we'll modify this instead.

To modify a text style:

1. On the **Text Styles** tab, right-click **Header and Footer** and select **Modify Header and Footer**.

2. In the **Text Style** dialog:

- From the **Character** category, select the **Font** sub-category.

- From the second **Font** drop-down list (displays **Websafe** by default), select **Favourites**.

- From the first **Font** drop-down list, select **Elementary SF**.

- From the **Text fill** drop-down list, select **Scheme Colour 1**.

- From the **Paragraph** category, select **Alignment and Spacing** sub-category.

- From the **Alignment** drop-down list, select **Right**.

- Click **OK**.

   Your copyright text updates to match the new settings.

3. Resize and reposition the text frame on the footer.

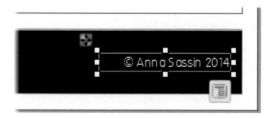

That's it! Your basic Master page design is complete.

Feel free to **Preview** your changes. (See p. 7 for details.)

We haven't discussed navigation bars, which generally appear on Master pages, in this tutorial. It is such an important feature of websites, we've got an entire tutorial dedicated to them. See the *Navigation bars and Sitemaps* tutorial starting on the following page for more details.

 Save your work by pressing **Ctrl+S.**

 You may wish to review your site development progress by checking the **Program Hints** section of the **Task Monitor** tab. Select any suggested processes you have completed and click **Mark as Fixed** to cross them off the list.

Navigation bars and Sitemaps

 45 min

Having fantastic content on your website is useless unless your visitors can get to it! Navigation bars are essential to successful site navigation. Luckily for us, WebPlus has a whole host of professionally designed dynamic navigation bars for us to use, and the process is easy.

By the end of this tutorial you will be able to:

- Change the design of an existing navigation bar.

- Customize a navigation bar.

- Add a navigation bar.

- Create a Sitemap.

> If you have already completed the *Master pages and Text Styles* tutorial on p. 15, you can use your saved project as the starting point for this tutorial.

Let's begin...

- Open the **WPX8 Tutorial 02.wpp** project file (see p. 16 for details).

> Alternatively, in the **Open** dialog, navigate to the folder where you saved your project file from the *Master pages and Text Styles* tutorial on p. 15, select it and click **Open**.

A site will open in the workspace with two pages, page guides and a basic Master page design.

Changing the style of an existing navigation bar

Generally, the main '**top level**' navigation bar is shared by all of the pages on a website. As a result, the navigation bar is usually placed on the Master page. This means that you only have to place the navigation bar once, even though it appears on each page.

So let's access the Master page in our site and begin work on the main navigation bar!

To access the master page:

1. On the **Pages** tab, click **Master Pages**.

2. Double-click the **Master A** thumbnail.

   The Master page is displayed in the workspace.

In our project file, the main navigation bar has become hidden by
our page design. We'll bring it to the front and place it on our
header panel.

To locate and reorder an object:

1. On the **Objects** tab:

- From the **Show** drop-down list, select **Navigation Bar**.

- Click ⊞ expand next to **Master A**.

- Click to select the displayed navigation bar.

2. On the **Arrange** toolbar, select 🗗 **Bring to Front**.

3. Drag the right central handle to the left to reduce the width of
the navigation bar.

4. With the navigation bar still selected, drag the object's  move button to position it neatly on the header panel. (We placed it top-right.)

The default navigation bar doesn't quite fit with our current design. Let's update the style of the navigation bar.

Save your work by pressing **Ctrl+S.**

To update the navigation bar style:

1. Double-click the navigation bar on the page.

2. In the **Edit Navigation Bar** dialog, select the **Type** tab.

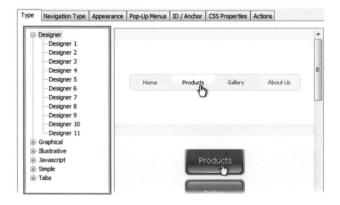

The category list (highlighted red) displays the available navigation bar categories. A preview is displayed in the main pane on the right.

3. From the **Designer** category, click to select the **Designer 2** navigation bar style.

A preview of the navigation bar appears on the right. (If you point to a part of the bar containing a pop-up menu the menu will also preview.)

4. Click **OK**.

The navigation bar is updated on the page.

 Save your work by pressing **Ctrl+S.**

Feel free to **Preview** your changes. (See p. 7 for details.)

The navigation bar matches better, but we can customize the bar further to fit our design.

Customizing a navigation bar

WebPlus hosts a dedicated studio which allows you to customize the buttons on your navigation bar to suit your specific needs. We'll explore this studio, as well as some of the other options in the **Edit Navigation Bar** dialog.

To customize navigation bar buttons in Button Studio:

1.   Double-click the navigation bar on the page.

2.   In the **Edit Navigation Bar** dialog, select the **Appearance** tab.

3.   From the categories on the left, select **Buttons**.

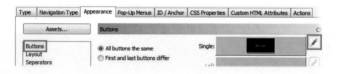

4.   Next to the **Single** design, click **Edit**.

The Button Studio opens. We'll update the text's font and colours within the design.

> For more details on using the Button Studio, see the studio's dedicated **How To** tab.

To update button text:

1. Click to select the text.

2. From the context toolbar, from the **Font** drop-down list, select **Elementary SF**.

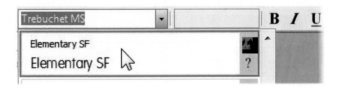

To update design colours:

1. On the **States** tab, double-click the **Down** state to display this state in the workspace.

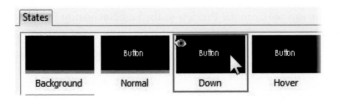

2. Click to select the lower rectangle on the page.

3. On the **Swatches** tab, select **Scheme Colour 1**.

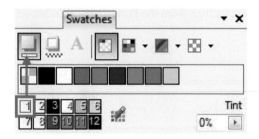

4. Repeat the steps 1-3 with the **Hover** state except, on the **Swatches** tab, select **Scheme Colour 10**.

5. On the **Standard** toolbar, click ✅ **Commit Changes**.

As you can see from the Preview in the Edit Navigation Bar dialog, the button text now matches our site text and buttons which are selected or 'hovered over' display as white or blue (scheme colour 1 or 10) rather than black (scheme colour 3).

The alignment of our navigation bar is currently set to Centre and Top. However, we've placed our navigation bar at the top right of our header (and page). We'll set our navigation bar's alignment to match our navigation bar's current position to keep our design neat.

To change navigation bar alignment:

1. In the **Edit Navigation Bar** dialog, select the **Appearance** tab.

2. From the categories on the left, select **Layout**.

3. From the **Horizontal Alignment** drop-down list, select **Right**.

4. Click **OK**.

The navigation bar updates on the page.

5. With the navigation bar still selected, drag the object's 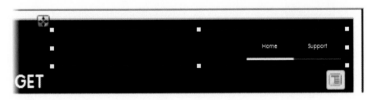 move button to position it neatly on the header panel. (We placed it top-right.)

Our customized design fits the look of our website better.

Save your work by pressing **Ctrl+S.**

Feel free to **Preview** your changes. (See p. 7 for details.)

Adding a navigation bar

Although our main site navigation is situated on the header, it's also a good idea to add site navigation to the bottom of your site so visitors have quick access if they're at the bottom of a page. Traditionally, this second navigation bar is less decorative. We'll add this new navigation bar to our footer.

To add a navigation bar:

1. On the **Quick Build** tab, in the **Navigation Items** category, click **Navigation Bar**.

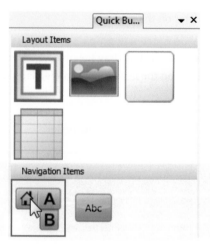

2. Position your cursor on the left of the footer panel and click once.

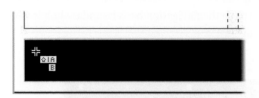

3. In the **Insert Navigation Bar** dialog:

- On the **Type** tab, from the **Simple** category, select **Simple 14**.

    Once you have selected a navigation bar style, other tabs will appear in the dialog.

- On the **Appearance** tab, from the categories on the left select **Layout**, and then from the **Horizontal Alignment** drop-down list, select **Left**.

4. Click **OK**.

The new navigation bar is added to the page, but extends beyond the page.

To resize a navigation bar:

● With the navigation bar still selected, drag the bottom right handle upwards so the navigation bar's boundary box is within the footer panel.

It is likely you will see a green exclamation mark appear because the bounding box is too small for the navigation bar. We'll customize this new navigation bar to ensure it fits neatly on our footer.

To customize navigation bar button sizes:

1. Double-click the navigation bar on the page.

2. In the **Edit Navigation Bar** dialog, select the **Appearance** tab.

3. From the categories on the left, select **Buttons**.

4. Next to the **Single** design, click 🖊 **Edit**.

5. In **Button Studio**:

- On the **States** tab, ensure the **Aspect Ratio** is **Locked** and then set the **W** (Width) to **40 pix**.

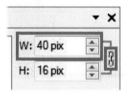

- Click to select the text.

- From the context toolbar, from the **Font** drop-down list, select **Elementary SF**.

- From the context toolbar, click **Colour** and select **Scheme Colour 1**.

- On the **Align** tab, click **Centre Horizontally** and **Centre Vertically**.

- Drag the central handles on the text boundary box inwards so the box sits neatly within the red guides.

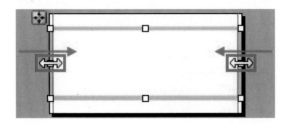

- On the **Standard** toolbar, click ✅ **Commit Changes**.

6. Back in the **Edit Navigation Bar** dialog, click **OK**.

The navigation bar updates to match our design and fits neatly within the boundary box. The green exclamation mark has vanished.

7. With the navigation bar still selected, drag the object's ✛ move button to position it neatly on the footer panel. (We placed it on the left.)

Now we have two sets of navigation objects on our site to help visitors access areas of our site.

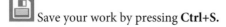 Save your work by pressing **Ctrl+S**.

Feel free to **Preview** your changes. (See p. 7 for details.)

Creating a Sitemap

A Sitemap is a special type of navigation element that displays every page in your site. It allows visitors to jump straight to any page and can help elevate your site's status within search engines.

First let's create a new blank page on which to place our Sitemap.

To add blank pages:

1. 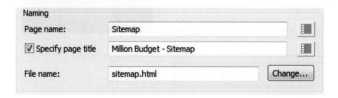 On the **Pages** tab, on the **Pages** panel, click the down arrow on the **Add new page or link** button and select **New Blank Page**.

2. In the **Page Properties** dialog:

Naming		
Page name:	Sitemap	
☑ Specify page title	Million Budget - Sitemap	
File name:	sitemap.html	Change...

   - In the **Page name** input box, drag to select the default name and then type 'Sitemap'.

   - Select the **Specify page title** option and update the contents of the adjacent input box.

- In the **File name** input box, drag to select the default name and then type 'sitemap.html'.

- In the **Placement** section, select **After** and then select **Support** from the drop-down list.

3. Click **OK**.

The new page is added to the site and displayed in the workspace and on the Pages tab. Our current navigation bars also update automatically.

Now let's add our Sitemap navigation bar to the page.

Save your work by pressing **Ctrl+S.**

To add a Sitemap navigation element:

1. On the **Pages** tab, double-click **Sitemap** to select it and display the page in the workspace.

2. On the **Quick Build** tab, in the **Navigation Items** category, click the **Navigation Bar** layout item.

3. Click once on the page.

4. In the **Insert Navigation Bar** dialog:

• On the **Type** tab, from the **Javascript** category, select **Javascript 1**.

  This design is perfect for a Sitemap because all child pages automatically display regardless of whether the parent pages are selected.

• Click **OK**.

5. Using the navigation bar's 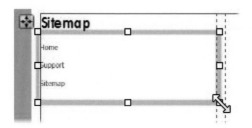 move button, drag to position it under the page name and drag the handles to display all the pages on the site.

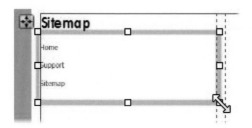

We can customize the design of this sitemap as well.

To customize a Sitemap:

1. Double-click the navigation bar on the page.

2. In the **Edit Navigation Bar** dialog, select the **Style** tab.

3. From the categories on the left, select **Level 1**.

4. On the right, double-click **Link Text Style** to edit the listed style.

5. In the **Link Text Style** dialog:

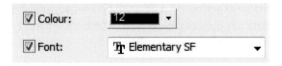

  - From the **Colour** drop-down list, select **Scheme Colour 12**.

  - From the **Font** drop-down list, select **Elementary SF**.

  - Click **OK**.

6. Repeat steps 4 and 5 to edit the **Non-link Text Style**.

7. On the right, double-click **Link Rollover Colour** and select **Scheme Colour 10**.

Your setup should now resemble ours...

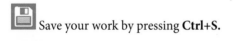

Name	Value
Link Text Style	Elementary SF;Scheme Colour 12 - Scheme Colour 12;
Non-link Text Style	Elementary SF;Scheme Colour 12 - Scheme Colour 12;
Link Rollover Colour	Scheme Colour 10 - Scheme Colour 10
Margin	L:0pix; T:15pix; R:0pix; B:15pix
Separator	None

8. Repeat steps 3-7 to edit the style for **Level 2**.

9. Click **OK**.

Your Sitemap page is now complete.

Save your work by pressing **Ctrl+S.**

Feel free to **Preview** your changes. (See p. 7 for details.)

Add and exclude pages from navigation bars

Traditionally links to a Sitemap do not appear in main navigation (or in the Sitemap itself). So to complete this tutorial, we will show you how to add and exclude pages from navigation bars.

To exclude a page from navigation bars:

1. With the Sitemap page still displayed in the workspace, on the context toolbar, click **Page Properties**.

2. In the **Page Properties** dialog:

   - On the left, select the **Navigation** category.

   - From the **Navigation** drop-down list, select **Exclude page from site navigation**.

   - Click **OK**.

All the navigation bars on the site update to exclude the Sitemap page. It also appears greyed-out with a cross beside it on the **Pages** tab.

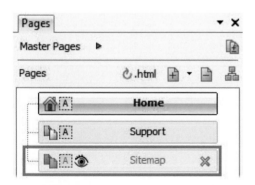

Now we'll re-add our Sitemap page to the navigation bar on our footer, to allow visitors to access the page.

To customize navigation bar structure:

1. On the **Pages** tab, click **Master Pages**.

2. Double-click the **Master A** thumbnail.

3. Double-click the navigation bar on the footer.

4. In the **Edit Navigation Bar** dialog, on the **Navigation Type** tab, select the **Custom** option.

By selecting the Custom option, you can now create an entirely bespoke navigation bar structure. This will no longer be linked to the site structure and will therefore need manually updating if more pages are added.

To create a custom navigation bar structure:

1. Click **Add Link**.

2. In the **Edit Hyperlink** dialog:

   • On the **Custom Navigation Tree Item** tab, in the **Menu name** input box, type 'Sitemap'.

   • Click the **Hyperlink** tab.

- On the **Hyperlink Type** tab, select the **Site Page** category.

- From the **Page name** drop-down list, select **Sitemap**.

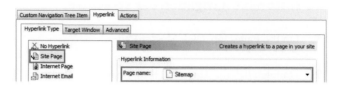

- Click **OK**.

  In the **Edit Navigation Bar** dialog, the custom navigation bar structure displays with the added link.

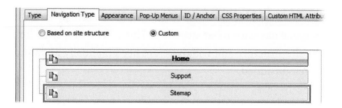

3. Click **OK**.

The selected navigation bar on the footer updates but the other navigation bars remain unchanged.

Feel free to **Preview** your changes. (See p. 7 for details.)

That's it! We've now explored some of the preset navigation bars available in WebPlus and how to customize them to suit your needs.

 Save your work by pressing **Ctrl+S.**

Sliders and text

30 min

The Home page is the first page visitors will see when they access your website. It is important that the page is both visually appealing and informative so as to catch a visitor's attention. A slider and frame text can help you achieve this dual goal of a Home page.

By the end of this tutorial you will be able to:

- Remove a Master page object from a single page.

- Add a blank slider to the page and resize a slider.

- Populate a slider using picture frames and pictures.

- Preview and customize slider animation.

- Add frame text.

If you have already completed the *Navigation bars and Sitemaps* tutorial on p. 39, you can use your saved project as the starting point for this tutorial.

Let's begin...

• Open the **WPX8 Tutorial 03.wpp** project file (see p. 16 for details).

 Alternatively, in the **Open** dialog, navigate to the folder where you saved your project file from the *Navigation bars and Sitemaps* tutorial on p. 39, select it and click **Open**.

A site will open in the workspace with three pages, page guides and a Master page design with navigation elements.

Removing Master page objects

Our Master page contains a page object which displays the current page's name just below the header. This is unnecessary for the Home page. So let's remove this object from the Home page without affecting other pages or the Master page design.

To remove Master page objects from a single site page:

1. On the **Pages** tab, double-click **Home** to select it and display the page in the workspace.

2. Click to select the Page name Master page object (currently displayed as **Home**). The object displays a unique toolbar.

3. Click 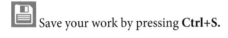 **Promote from Master Page**.

The object remains in the same place on the page but is no longer attached to the Master page in this instance.

4. Click to select the border of the text frame and press the **Delete** key.

Now we'll begin our Home page design using a slider.

Save your work by pressing **Ctrl+S.**

Adding a blank slider to a page

If you want to add a new slider to your site, you'll find many different types of slider in the **Assets Browser** ready to be added to your page and customized to suit your requirements. However, for full design freedom, you can add a blank slider to the page.

To add a slider to the page:

1. On the **Quick Build** tab, in the **Interactive Objects** category, hold the **Ctrl** key down and click the **Slider** layout item.

2. Click on the page.

The empty slider is added at a default size.

3. With the slider still selected, drag the object's 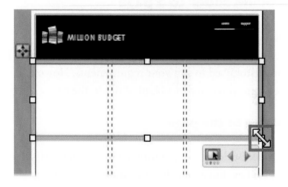 move button to position it alongside the top and left margin guides.

Next, we'll explore various ways in which you can resize your slider.

To resize a slider on the page:

1. Click on the slider to select it.

2. Drag the bottom-right corner handle to resize the slider.

Hold down the **Shift** key as you drag to maintain the slider's aspect ratio

Alternatively, you can set a specific size for the slider using the Transform tab.

To resize a slider using the Transform tab:

1. Click on the slider to select it.

2. On the **Transform** tab:

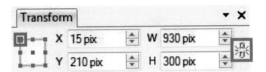

- Ensure the object is set to **Anchor Top Left** and the **Aspect Ratio** is **Unlocked**.

- Set **W** (Width) to **930 pix** and **H** (Height) to **300 pix**.

Now let's look at some ways in which we can populate the slider.

 Save your work by pressing **Ctrl+S**.

Populating a slider

There are virtually endless uses for sliders. They can be used to display photos (as a sliding gallery), for advertising banners, animated navigation elements, dated and timed promotions, and much more.

We're going to walk you through a basic design which scrolls through pictures which depict the work of our company.

We'll do all our work in the dedicated Slider Studio.

To access the Slider Studio:

1. Click on the slider to select it.

2. On the context toolbar, click 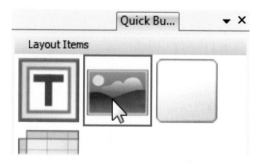 **Slider Studio**.

The Slider Studio opens, displaying the first panel of your slider in the workspace. We'll begin our design using a framed picture.

To add a framed picture:

1. On the **Quick Build** tab, in the **Layout Items** category, hold the **Ctrl** key down and click the **Picture** layout item.

2. Click on the panel in the workspace.

The empty picture frame is added at a default size. We'll resize and position this precisely using the Transform tab.

To resize a picture frame using the Transform tab:

1. Click on the picture frame to select it.

2. On the **Transform** tab:

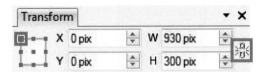

- Ensure the object is set to **Anchor Top Left** and the **Aspect Ratio** is **Unlocked**.

- Set **X** to **0 pix** and **Y** to **0 pix**.

- Set **W** (Width) to **930 pix** and **H** (Height) to **300 pix**.

The picture frame resizes to fill the entire panel.

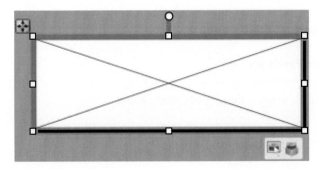

Before we fill this with a picture, we'll replicate the panel.

To replicate slider panels:

- On the **Panels** tab:

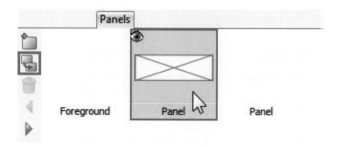

- Click to select the first **Panel**.

- Click ![] **Copy Slider Panel**.

We now have three panels in total, one blank and the other two with a picture frame each. We'll remove the blank panel.

To remove a slider panel:

- On the **Panels** tab:

  - Click to select the second (blank) **Panel**.

  - Click ![] **Delete Slider Panel**.

Next we'll add pictures to our frames. We'll show you the two ways you can do this.

To add a picture from file:

1. Click to select the picture frame on the panel.

2. On the object toolbar, click **Replace Picture from File**.

3. In the **Import Picture** dialog, browse to your **Images** folder.

In a standard installation, the image files can be accessed from the following location:

C:\Program Files\Serif\WebPlus\X8\Images or
C:\Program Files (x86)\Serif\WebPlus\X8\Images

However, the path may differ if you changed the installation location.

4. Select **060510n0046.JPG** and click **Open**.

The picture is added to the frame and scaled to maximum-fit by default.

You can also add (or replace) a picture within a frame directly using a Picture asset.

We've provided a convenient Tutorial asset pack which contains all the pictures you will need to help you progress through this tutorial.

To add a Picture asset to a frame:

1. On the **Panels** tab, double-click the other **Panel** to display it in the workspace.

2. Click to select the picture frame on the panel.

3. On the object toolbar, click  **Replace Picture from Assets**.

4. In the **Asset Browser**:

   - From the **Tutorials** category, select the photo of the two businesswomen.

   - Click **OK**.

The picture is added to the frame and scaled to maximum-fit by default. The default position applies an unfortunate crop, which we'll fix next.

To reposition the picture inside the frame:

1. Click to select the picture.

2. On the object toolbar, click  **Position Image**, and drag on the picture to position it better.

> Feel free to experiment with the other adjustments on the Picture Frame toolbar. See *Adding picture frames* in WebPlus Help for details.

Next we'll look at the unique properties of the Foreground panel.

Using the Foreground panel

All sliders contain a Foreground panel, which you can use at your discretion. Any objects added to the Foreground panel will appear on top of all the content placed on other slider panels.

We'll add some content to the Foreground panel to show you how it works.

To add content to the Foreground panel (QuickShape):

1. On the **Panels** tab, double-click the **Foreground** panel to display it in the workspace.

2. On the **Drawing** toolbar, from the QuickShape flyout, select **Quick Rectangle**.

3. Click anywhere on the panel to add a rectangle at the default size.

4. On the **Transform** tab:

   - Ensure the object is set to **Anchor Top Left**.

   - Set **X** to **40 pix** and **Y** to **40 pix**.

   - Set **W** (Width) to **220 pix** and **H** (Height) to **220 pix**.

5. On the **Swatches** tab:

- Set the 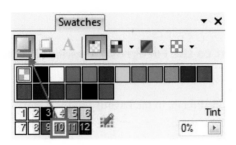 **Fill** to **Scheme Colour 10**.

- Click 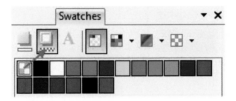 **Line** and set this to **None**.

6. On the **Transparency** tab:

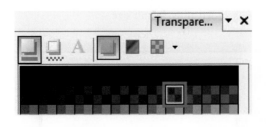

- Click **Fill**.

- Select the **Solid Transparency 40%** swatch. (Names appear as tooltips.)

The first stage of our Foreground panel design is now complete.

Next, we'll add text.

To add content to the Foreground panel (Frame Text):

1. On the **Quick Build** tab, in the **Layout Items** category, click the **Text Frame** layout item.

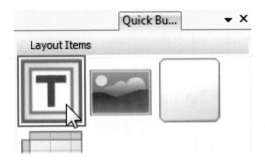

2. Click anywhere inside the coloured square on the panel.

The text frame is added at its default size.

A flashing cursor will indicate the text frame is ready for you to type (or paste) text.

3. On the context toolbar, from the **Style** drop-down list, select **Heading 2**.

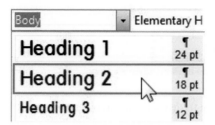

4. Type 'Welcome...' and then press the **Return** key.

5. From the **Text** menu, select **Insert>Fill with Placeholder Text**. Alternatively, feel free to add your own welcome text.

6. Select the edge of the text frame and hold down the **Shift** key and click to select the coloured square also.

7. On the **Align** tab:

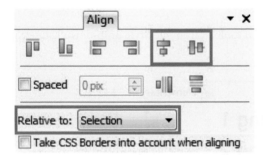

- From the **Relative to** drop-down list, select **Selection**.

- Click  **Centre Horizontally** and **Centre Vertically**.

Our Foreground panel design is now complete.

Let's preview our slider within Slider Studio and adjust the slider options to suit our needs.

The foreground panel is a great place to put information that you always want people to see. Examples of its use could be for contact information, a button or a watermark. As the foreground panel itself cannot be animated, you could add a picture to it. This way you can use a single image with animated text panels. You'll find examples of different kinds of sliders in the **Asset Browser**.

Previewing and modifying options in Slider Studio

Let's see how our design looks and how the Foreground panel interacts with the other panels.

To preview a slider in Slider Studio:

* On the **Standard** toolbar, click ⬚ **Preview**.

The Slider Studio will switch to Preview mode and your slider will rotate between the two panels displaying our pictures. The coloured rectangle and frame text will appear continuously over the top as they are on the Foreground panel.

The default transitions are a little abrupt, so let's create a smoother transition for our panels.

To adjust panel transitions:

* On the **Slider Options** tab:

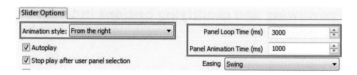

* From the **Animation style** drop-down list, select **From the right**.

* Set the **Panel Loop Time (ms)** to **3000**.

* Set the **Panel Animation Time (ms)** to **1000**.

The slider will now take longer to cycle through each panel and the transition time is doubled. Panels will now slide in from the right rather than flicking between each other.

 Feel free to adjust the settings to suit your needs and experiment with the other options on the panel. See *Inserting Sliders* in WebPlus Help for more details of the available settings.

 If you wish to modify the slider content, on the context toolbar, click **Return to Editor**.

To exit Slider Studio:

* On the **Standard** toolbar, click  **Close Studio**.

Back in the WebPlus workspace, your slider design has updated to reflect the changes made in the Slider Studio. Next, we'll add text to our Home page to complete the design.

Save your work by pressing **Ctrl+S.**

Adding text

To make your site as accessible as possible, you should use text frames for all main body text content. These are added to the page in an identical way to how we added them to our Foreground panel on our slider.

To place and populate a text frame:

1. On the **Quick Build** tab, in the **Layout Items** category, click the **Text Frame** layout item.

2. Click anywhere on the page.

3. On the **Transform** tab:

* Ensure the object is set to **Anchor Top Left** and the **Aspect Ratio** is **Unlocked**.

* Set **X** to **15 pix** and **Y** to **525 pix**.

* Set **W** (Width) to **300 pix** and **H** (Height) to **385 pix**.

4. On the context toolbar, from the **Style** drop-down list, select **Heading 3**.

5. Type 'Who are we?' and then press the **Return** key.

6. From the **Text** menu, select **Insert>Fill with Placeholder Text**. Alternatively, feel free to add your own custom text.

We'll add another text frame to our Home page by using another placement method.

We can align this new text frame with our first text frame using dynamic guides.

 Dynamic guides allow you to align new objects to the last three selected page objects.

To use dynamic guides:

• On the **Arrange** toolbar:

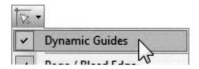

• Ensure **Snapping** is enabled.

• From the **Snapping** flyout, ensure **Dynamic Guides** is enabled.

Now, we'll create a new text frame and align it to the guides which appear on the page.

To add a text frame:

1. On the **Basic** toolbar, select  **Insert Text Frame**.

2. Position the cursor on the left of the middle column. The red dynamic guide will help you align your cursor with the text frame to the left.

3. Drag down and to the right to place a text frame which fills the middle column.

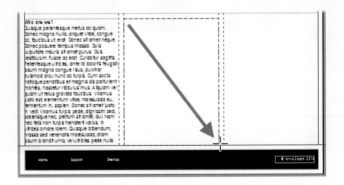

4. On the context toolbar, from the **Style** drop-down list, select **Heading 3**.

5. Type 'How can we help?' and then press the **Return** key.

6. From the **Text** menu, select **Insert>Fill with Placeholder Text**. Alternatively, feel free to add your own custom text.

That's it! Our Home page design is complete. We're going to leave the third column empty so we can use the space in the *Linking to social media* tutorial on p. 119.

 Feel free to **Preview** your changes. (See p. 7 for details.)

 Save your work by pressing **Ctrl+S**.

Forms, User Details and Google maps

 30 min

In this tutorial we'll explore many of the contact options you can offer to visitors, including a contact form and Google map.

By the end of this tutorial you will be able to:

- Add a contact form.

    - Customize a contact form.

    - Set up form submission using Serif Web Resources.

- Add telephone and email User Details.

- Add a Google map.

> If you have already completed the *Sliders and text* tutorial on p. 63, you can use your saved project as the starting point for this tutorial.

Let's begin...

* Open the **WPX8 Tutorial 04.wpp** project file (see p. 16 for details).

> Alternatively, in the **Open** dialog, navigate to the folder where you saved your project file from the *Sliders and text* tutorial on p. 63, select it and click **Open**.

A partially designed site will open in the workspace.

The Contact page is arguably the most important page on your website. Many visitors will use your website to find a way of getting in touch with you. We recommend offering as many contact avenues as possible. We'll start with a contact form.

Adding a contact form

A contact form is a convenient way for visitors to get in touch with you. It is particularly useful if you are reticent on displaying your phone number or email address directly on your site.

WebPlus comes with preset forms which you can quickly add to your page and modify to meet your needs. We'll add a contact form to our blank Support page.

To add a contact form to the page:

1. On the **Pages** tab, double-click **Support** to select it and display the page in the workspace.

2. On the **Quick Build** tab, click the **Forms** header, and then click the **Form** item.

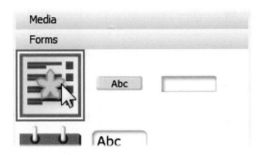

3. Click anywhere on the page.

The Form Designer dialog opens.

4. On the **Templates** tab, from the **Form Templates** list, select **Comments 1**.

The current form design displays in the preview on the right.

5. On the **Form** tab's **Form Properties** tab:

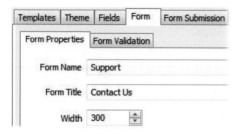

- In the **Form Name** input box, type 'Support'.

- In the **Form Title** input box, type 'Contact Us'.

- Set the **Width** to **300**.

    The preview on the right updates to reflect the changes.

6. Click **OK**.

7. You will receive a message informing you that your form has no action set. We will discuss this on p. 93, so for now click **OK**.

    The form is added to the page.

8. On the **Transform** tab:

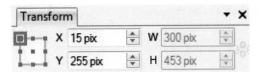

- Ensure the object is set to **Anchor Top Left**.

- Set **X** to **15 pix** and **Y** to **255 pix**.

The form contains the contact fields we need, but does not fit our current site's design. We'll modify this next.

Save your work by pressing **Ctrl+S**.

Feel free to **Preview** your changes. (See p. 7 for details.)

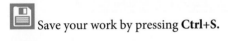

Customizing a form

To customize the form we'll use the scheme colours and fonts already using in our site.

To speed up your design process, you can add any fonts to a customizable **Favourites** category. See p. 27 for more information.

Now, onto customizing the contact form...

To customize a form:

1. Double-click the form on the page.

The Form Designer dialog opens.

2. On the **Theme** tab's **Customize Form** tab:

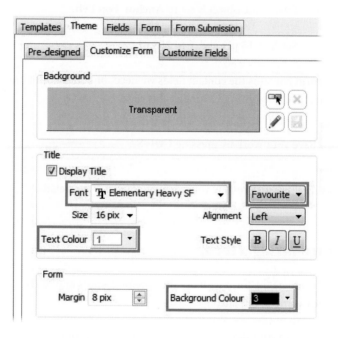

- From the second **Font** drop-down list (displays **Websafe** by default), select **Favourites**.

- From the first **Font** drop-down list, select **Elementary Heavy SF**.

- From the **Text Colour** drop-down list, select **Scheme Colour 1**.

- From the **Background Colour** drop-down list, select **Scheme Colour 3**.

3. On the **Theme** tab's **Customize Fields** tab, in the **Label** section:

- From the second **Font** drop-down list (displays **Websafe** by default), select **Favourites**.

- From the first **Font** drop-down list, select **Elementary SF**.

- From the **Size** drop-down list, select **12 pix**.

- From the **Text Colour** drop-down list, select **Scheme Colour 1**.

4. In the **Input Element** section, repeat step 3, except from the **Text Colour** drop-down list, select **Scheme Colour 12**.

5. In the **Buttons** section:

- From the **Text Colour** drop-down list, select **Scheme Colour 12**.

- From the **Background** drop-down list, select **Scheme Colour 10**.

  The preview on the right updates to reflect the changes.

6. Click **OK**.

7. You will receive a message informing you that your form has no action set. We will discuss this next, so for now click **OK**.

The form is updated on the page.

Save your work by pressing **Ctrl+S.**

Feel free to **Preview** your changes. (See p. 7 for details.)

Form submission via Serif Web Resources

We recommend using Serif Web Resources as the destination for data submission. Serif Web Resources will collect the data and then send it to a specified email address.

To use Serif Web Resources to collect data:

1. Double-click the form on the page.

The Form Designer dialog opens.

2. On the **Form Submission** tab:

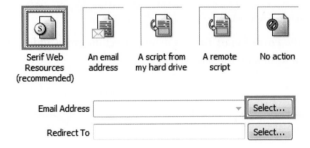

- Select **Serif Web Resources**.

- Next to the **Email Address** field, click **Select**.

   If you're logged into Serif Web Resources, the Form Email Targets dialog will open. This allows you to set the email address which data will be sent to.

If you are not logged into Serif Web Resources, you'll be presented with the
Serif Web Resources Login dialog.

Enter your **Username** and **Password** then click **Login**.

If you don't have a Serif Web Resources account, you can sign up by adding
details to the **New User?** Section and clicking **Signup**.

3. In the **Form Email Targets** dialog, select the email address you
used to sign up for Serif Web Resources.

 If you wish for data to be sent to another email address, in the **Add new**
section, type the email address and click **Add new**.

An email with an activation link will be sent to the email address stated.
When the link in the email has been clicked, the email address will be able
to receive data from this form.

4. Back on the **Form Submission** tab, from the **Confirmation Field** drop-down list, select **Email** and then click **Format**.

5. In the **Email Format** dialog:

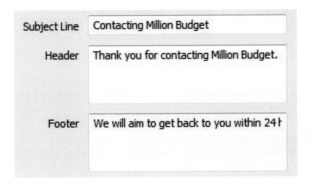

- In the **Subject Line** input box, type the subject of the email which can be read from the visitor's email inbox.

- Type an optional **Header** and **Footer**. The Header text appears in the body of the email before a list of the data submitted, while the Footer text appears after the list.

- Click **OK**.

6. Click **OK** to return to the WebPlus workspace.

We have now set the form submission via Serif Web Resources. This means that when a visitor fills in the form, the data is sent via Serif Web Resources to the email address selected.

To protect yourself from receiving spam from your form, Serif Web Resources will automatically redirect visitors to a page where they will need to complete a reCAPTCHA™ field before the data from the form is submitted. Alternatively, you can add your own CAPTCHA or reCAPTCHA™ field to the bottom of the form. For details, see *Form field properties* in WebPlus Help.

Save your work by pressing **Ctrl+S.**

Feel free to **Preview** your changes. (See p. 7 for details.)

You can test the form works by filling out the fields and adding your own email address before clicking **Submit.**

You may wish to review your site development progress by checking the **Program Hints** section of the **Task Monitor** tab. Select any suggested processes you have completed and click **Mark as Fixed** to cross them off the list.

Adding User Details

Rather than using a form, visitors may be interested in contacting you directly via telephone or email. You can add these details to your page using a text frame and User Details.

To add a text frame:

1. On the **Quick Build** tab, in the **Layout Items** category, click the **Text Frame** layout item.

2. Position the cursor below the contact form and drag on the page to create a text frame which spans the first column.

To add User Details:

1. With the text frame still selected, from the **Text** menu, click **Insert>Information>User Details**.

2. In the **User Details** dialog:

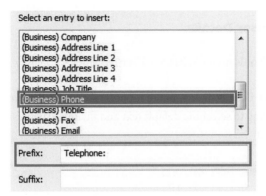

* From the entry list, select **(Business) Phone**.

* In the **Prefix** input box, type 'Telephone: '.

* Click **OK**.

  The user detail field is added to the text frame.

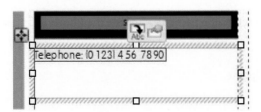

3. Press the **Return** key and then repeat the above steps to add another user detail field for the **(Business) Email** with a prefix of 'Email: '.

The user details which currently display use the default settings. We will update these to match our company.

To update User Details:

1. From the **Tools** menu, select **Set User Details**.

2. In the **User Details** dialog, in the input boxes on the **Business Sets** tab, drag to select the default text and then type your custom text.

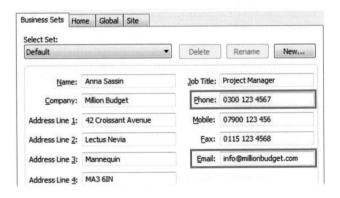

For this tutorial in particular, update the **Phone** and **Email** fields.

3. Click **Update**.

Your custom user details are updated on the page.

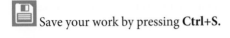Save your work by pressing **Ctrl+S.**

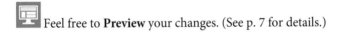Feel free to **Preview** your changes. (See p. 7 for details.)

Adding a Google map

To complete our page design, we're going to provide visitors with a
map so they can locate the company premises easily, if needed.

To insert a Google map:

1. On the **Quick Build** tab, in the **Interactive Objects** category,
   click the **Google Map** layout item.

2. Position the cursor in line with the top of the contact form.

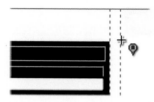

3. Drag down to the right so the map fills the remaining space on the page.

4. In the **Insert Google Map** dialog:

- In the **Search for a location** input box, type the location you wish to appear at the centre of the map.

- Click **Search**.

    The map on the right will update to show the searched location.

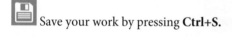
Navigate around the map using regular panning and zoom controls—drag the hand cursor to pan, the zoom slider and buttons to magnify/zoom out.

- Click **OK**.

The Google map is added to the page showing the location set in the dialog.

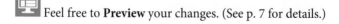 Save your work by pressing **Ctrl+S.**

Feel free to **Preview** your changes. (See p. 7 for details.)

To improve our map, we'll add a marker to inform visitors precisely where the company is located.

To add a marker:

1. Double-click the map on the page.

2. In the **Edit Google Map** dialog, in the **Map Markers** section, click **Add**.

3. In the **Google Map Marker** dialog:

- Click a chosen location using the $^{-}_{\,|}{}^{-}$ cursor.

- In the **Name** input box, type the name of the company. This "tooltip" displays on hover over.

- In the **Label** input box, type the company address.

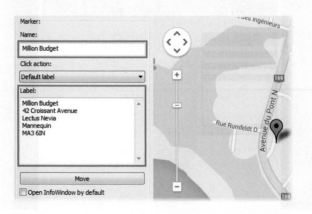

Select the **Open InfoWindow by default** option if you wish your Label to display without the marker being clicked.

- Click **OK**.

   The marker appears on the map preview in green (to indicate it is currently selected).

4. Back in the **Edit Google Map** dialog, click **OK**.

The map updates on the page.

That's it! Our contact page design is complete. Now visitors can get in touch with you via a contact form, telephone, and email and locate your business on a map.

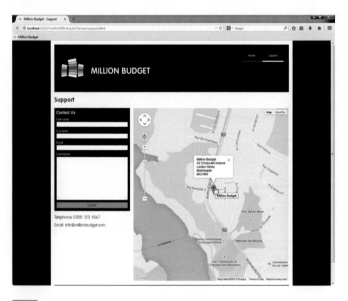 Feel free to **Preview** your changes. (See p. 7 for details.)

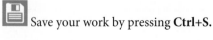 Save your work by pressing **Ctrl+S.**

Using hyperlinks

 15 min

WebPlus provides a wide and very flexible range of hyperlink options. This means easy navigation for your site's visitors—and possibly a more efficient visit if your site includes large pictures.

By the end of this tutorial you will be able to:

- Create a link to a site page.

- Create anchors.

- Create a hyperlink to an anchor.

- Create a link to the top of the page.

- Create external hyperlinks to a social media account.

> If you have already completed the *Forms, User Details and Google maps* tutorial on p. 85, you can use your saved project as the starting point for this tutorial.

Let's begin...

- Open the **WPX8 Tutorial 05.wpp** project file (see p. 16 for details).

Alternatively, in the **Open** dialog, navigate to the folder where you saved your project file from the *Forms, User Details and Google maps* tutorial on p. 85, select it and click **Open**.

A partially designed site will open in the workspace.

Hyperlinks are an effective way of navigating around websites.

Almost any object on your page can have a hyperlink assigned to it or can be the destination for a hyperlink.

Let's jump straight in and set up a hyperlink to a site page.

Creating a link to a site page using text

Navigation bars are generally used for jumping between pages within a website. See the *Navigation bars and Sitemaps* tutorial on p. 39 for more information on navigation bars. However, there may be times when you refer to a site page in your text and want to link to it there. This can be achieved using a hyperlink.

To create a link to a site page:

1. On the **Basic** toolbar, select ![pointer] **Pointer Tool**.

2. Click anywhere in the second text frame on the Home page and then drag to select the words 'How can we help?'.

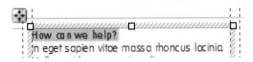

3. On the **Properties** toolbar, select ![hyperlink] **Hyperlink**.

4. In the **Edit Hyperlink** dialog:

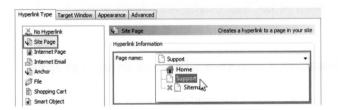

- On the **Hyperlink Type** tab, select the **Site Page** category.

- From the **Page name** drop-down list, select **Support**.

- Click **OK**.

The text is converted into a hyperlink.

 Save your work by pressing **Ctrl+S**.

A dedicated object toolbar displays allowing you to edit and remove the hyperlink.

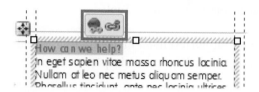

Feel free to **Preview** your changes. (See p. 7 for details.)

When your mouse is positioned over the hyperlink, a new cursor displays to indicate that clicking will redirect you to another page location.

How can we help?
In eget sapie vitae massa rhoncus lacinic
Nullam at leo nec metus aliquam semper

Creating a link to a site page using a graphic

You can also place a hyperlink on a picture or graphic to allow people to navigate around your site. Traditionally, if you have a logo on your site header, this will link to the Home page of your site. Let's set this up next...

To access the master page:

1. On the **Pages** tab, click **Master Pages**.

2. Double-click the **Master A** thumbnail.

   The Master page is displayed in the workspace.

To create a link to a site page:

1. On the **Basic** toolbar, select 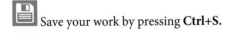 **Pointer Tool**.

2. Click to select the logo on the header.

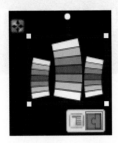

3. On the **Properties** toolbar, select 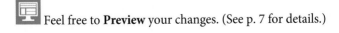 **Hyperlink**.

4. In the **Edit Hyperlink** dialog:

- On the **Hyperlink Type** tab, select the **Site Page** category.

- From the **Page name** drop-down list, select **Home**.

- Click **OK**.

The logo now contains a hyperlink.

Save your work by pressing **Ctrl+S**.

Feel free to **Preview** your changes. (See p. 7 for details.)

When your mouse is positioned over the hyperlink, a new cursor displays to indicate that clicking will redirect you to another page location.

Adding anchors

Anchors act as fixed points on your site which you can link to. Anchors must be created first before a hyperlink can be established to it.

We'll create an anchor on our Support page.

To add an anchor:

1. On the **Pages** tab, from the **Pages** pane, double-click the **Support** page.

2. On the **Basic** toolbar, select **Pointer Tool**.

3. Click to select the telephone user detail in the text frame.

4. On the **Properties** toolbar, click 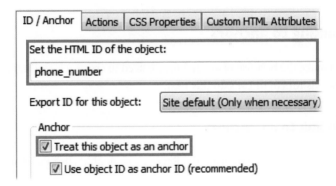 **ID and Anchor**.

5. In the **Edit Text Frame** dialog, on the **ID/Anchor** tab:

ID / Anchor	Actions	CSS Properties	Custom HTML Attributes

Set the HTML ID of the object:

phone_number

Export ID for this object: Site default (Only when necessary)

Anchor

☑ Treat this object as an anchor

☑ Use object ID as anchor ID (recommended)

- In the **Set the HTML ID of the object** input box, replace the default name with something easier to remember. We used 'phone_number'.

> We recommend that all HTML names remain in lower case and do not contain spaces.

- Select the **Treat this object as an anchor** option.

- Click **OK**.

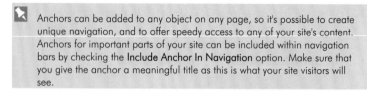

Anchors can be added to any object on any page, so it's possible to create unique navigation, and to offer speedy access to any of your site's content. Anchors for important parts of your site can be included within navigation bars by checking the **Include Anchor In Navigation** option. Make sure that you give the anchor a meaningful title as this is what your site visitors will see.

We now have an anchor which specifically identifies our telephone number on the Support page. This is indicated by the icon on the object toolbar.

Save your work by pressing **Ctrl+S.**

Linking to anchors

To make the best use of an anchor, we need to create a hyperlink to take visitors to it! Let's do this next.

To link to an anchor:

1. On the **Pages** tab, from the **Pages** pane, double-click the **Home** page.

2. On the **Basic** toolbar, select **Pointer Tool**.

3. Click anywhere in the second text frame and then drag to select the final sentence.

4. On the **Properties** toolbar, select **Hyperlink**.

5. In the **Edit Hyperlink** dialog:

- On the **Hyperlink Type** tab, select the **Anchor** category.

- From the **Page name** drop-down list, select **Support**.

- From the **Anchor** drop-down list, select your previously created anchor.

- Click **OK**.

The text now hyperlinks to telephone number on the Support page.

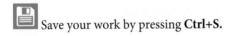 Save your work by pressing **Ctrl+S.**

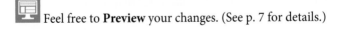 Feel free to **Preview** your changes. (See p. 7 for details.)

Our pages aren't particularly long, so the difference between linking to this anchor and the entire page is subtle. However, you may notice that when using the 'How can we help?' text link the Support page displays with the header fully visible, whereas the text linking to the anchor displays the footer fully on the Support page.

Creating 'to top' hyperlinks

For long web pages you may want to offer a link back to the top of
the page.

To add assets to the Assets tab:

1. On the **Pages** tab, click **Master Pages**, and then double-click the
Master A thumbnail.

2. On the **Assets** tab, click  **Browse** to open the **Asset
Browser**.

3. In the **Asset Browser**, select the **Page Content** category.

4. In the search box (top-right of the dialog), type 'back to top'.

As you type, the assets in the gallery will reduce down.

5. Click to select a button of your choice from the **Back to Top** sub-category of the **Page Content** category. We chose the white arrow on a clear background.

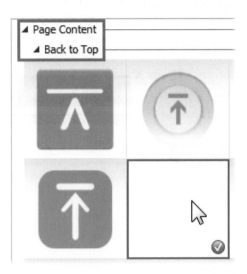

The green shows the asset will be added to the **Assets** tab.

6. Click **Close** to exit the dialog and return to the page.

The button is displayed in the **Assets** tab.

Next, we'll add this button to the page.

To add a button to the page:

1. On the **Assets** tab, the **Page Content** category should be displayed (if not, click the header).

2. Drag the button onto the page.

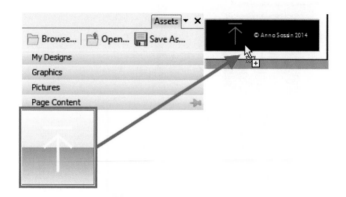

3. On the **Transform** tab:

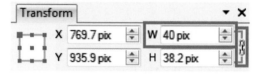

- Ensure the **Aspect Ratio** is **Locked**.

- Set **W** (Width) to **40 pix**.

4. Reposition the button and the copyright text so the 'to top' arrow is on the footer's far right.

Next, we'll add a hyperlink to our button.

To create a 'top' link:

1. Select the 'to top' button.

2. On the **Properties** toolbar, select  **Hyperlink**.

3. In the **Edit Button** dialog, on the **Hyperlink** tab:

- On the **Hyperlink Type** tab, select the **Internet Page** category.

- In the **URL address** input box, type '#top'.

- On the **Target Window** tab, from the **Type** drop-down list, select **Same Window**.

- Click **OK**.

On all pages which use the Master page, a visitor can use the arrow to return to the top of the page instantly.

Save your work by pressing **Ctrl+S.**

 Feel free to **Preview** your changes. (See p. 7 for details.)

Creating an external hyperlink to Twitter

For this final section, we'll look at setting up a hyperlink which links to an external website on the internet.

To add an external hyperlink:

1. On the **Pages** tab, from the **Pages** pane, double-click the **Support** page.

2. On the **Basic** toolbar, select ![pointer] **Pointer Tool**.

3. Click to select the text frame below the form and then increase the height of the frame (if necessary).

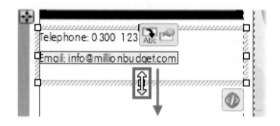

4. Click to place the cursor at the end of the email address and then press the **Return** key.

5. Type in 'Twitter: @millionbudget' and then drag to select '@millionbudget'.

6. On the **Properties** toolbar, select 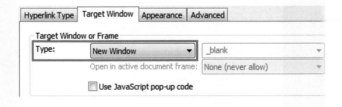 **Hyperlink**.

7. In the **Edit Hyperlink** dialog:

- On the **Hyperlink Type** tab, select the **Internet Page** category.

- In the **URL address** input box, type 'https://twitter.com/millionbudget'.

- On the **Target Window** tab, from the **Type** drop-down list, select **New Window**.

Hyperlink Type	Target Window	Appearance	Advanced

Target Window or Frame

Type:	New Window ▼	_blank ▼
	Open in active document frame:	None (never allow) ▼

☐ Use JavaScript pop-up code

- Click **OK**.

By setting the Target Window to New Window, this will ensure a new window (or tab) is opened in the visitor's browser when the link is clicked. This will mean your website remains open in the browser for visitors to get back to quickly once they have finished browsing the external website.

That's it! You now have a variety of hyperlinks on your site to help visitors move around efficiently. Remember, you can add hyperlinks to virtually any page object and can link to a huge variety of locations.

> You can link to social media throughout your website to fully promote your company, club, charity, or personal activities. We look at ways you can do this in the *Linking to social media* tutorial on the following pages.

Feel free to **Preview** your changes. (See p. 7 for details.)

 Save your work by pressing **Ctrl+S.**

Linking to social media

 15 min

Social media can be great for growing a business or promoting a company, charity, or club. This tutorial explores some of the ways you can link your site to social media platforms or enable visitors to actively shout about your website with ease!

By the end of this tutorial you will be able to:

- Add a Facebook Like feed.

- Add a Pinterest pin to a picture.

- Add Facebook, Twitter, and Google+ recommendation buttons.

- Add a bookmarking button strip.

 If you have already completed the *Using hyperlinks* tutorial on p. 103, you can use your saved project as the starting point for this tutorial.

Let's begin...

- Open the **WPX8 Tutorial 06.wpp** project file (see p. 16 for details).

Alternatively, in the **Open** dialog, navigate to the folder where you saved your project file from the *Using hyperlinks* tutorial on p. 103, select it and click **Open**.

A partially designed site will open in the workspace.

Adding a Facebook Like feed

A Facebook Like feed allows visitors to recommend your Facebook page while at the same time displaying its most recent posts. This is a great way of linking your website to your social media activity and ensures anything you post on Facebook immediately appears on your website!

We'll place our feed on the Home page, as this will keep the content fresh for returning visitors.

To add a Facebook widget:

1. On the **Quick Build** tab, in the **Social Media** category, click **Facebook Widget**.

2. Click once in the empty column on the page.

3. In the **Insert Facebook Widget** dialog, on the **Facebook Widget** tab:

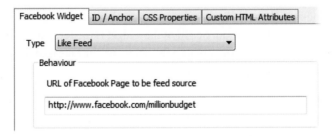

- From the **Type** drop-down list, select **Like Feed**.

- In the **URL of Facebook Page to be feed source** input box, type the web address for your Facebook page.

- Click **OK**.

  The Facebook Like feed is added to the page.

If nothing appears in the Facebook widget, double-click the Like Feed and check that the URL of Facebook Page is correct.

4. On the **Transform** tab:

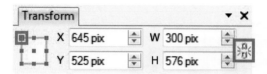

- Ensure the object is set to **Anchor Top Left** and the **Aspect Ratio** is **Unlocked**.

- Set **X** to **645 pix** and **Y** to **525 pix**.

- Set **W** (Width) to **300 pix**.

Although we have widened and repositioned our Like feed, the recommended minimum height of the widget is too long to fit our current page. Rather than reduce the height of our Like feed, we'll increase the height of our page.

Save your work by pressing **Ctrl+S.**

To increase the height of a page:

1. Hover the cursor at the bottom of the page until it changes to show a double-headed arrow.

2. Drag downwards to increase the height (length) of the page until the bottom of the widget fits neatly against the bottom blue margin.

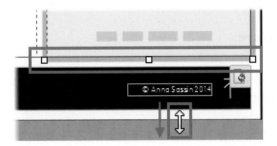

Our page now neatly accommodates the Facebook Like feed.

 Feel free to **Preview** your changes. (See p. 7 for details.)

Pinning a picture

You can add a Pinterest pin to any picture on your site to allow visitors to pin it to their Pinterest account and share it with their Pinterest followers. We'll show you how using the pictures on our slider.

> ⚠ Due to Google Chrome's in-built pop-up blocker, visitors to your site who use Chrome may not be able to see the Pinterest pin.

To pin a picture:

1. Click to select the slider at the top of the Home page and on the object's toolbar, click **Show Next Panel**.

2. Click to select the picture on the slider panel.

3. On the **Properties** toolbar, select 🞕 **Edit actions**.

4. In the **Edit Picture** dialog, on the **Actions** tab, click **Add** and then select **Pinterest** from the drop-down list.

5. In the **Pinterest Action** dialog, click **OK**.

   Pinterest is added to the picture's list of actions.

6. Click **OK**.

7. With the picture still select, on the object's toolbar, click **Select Parent** to select the slider panel and then click **Show Next Panel**.

8. Repeat steps 2-6 to add a pin to the second picture on the slider.

Now, when a visitor positions their mouse cursor over the pictures on the slider a Pinterest pin will appear in the top left corner. When the **Pin it** button is clicked, the visitor will add the picture to their Pinterest collection and it will be seen by their followers.

 Save your work by pressing **Ctrl+S**.

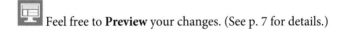 Feel free to **Preview** your changes. (See p. 7 for details.)

Adding recommendation buttons

Social media is a great way of spreading the word about your website. WebPlus includes widgets which allow users to recommend your website on Facebook, Twitter, and Google+. We'll add these to our Support page.

To add a Twitter Follow button:

1. On the **Pages** tab, double-click **Support** to select it and display the page in the workspace.

2. On the **Quick Build** tab, in the **Social Media** category, click **Twitter Widget**.

3. Click once under the text frame containing the telephone, email, and twitter details.

4. In the **Insert Twitter Widget** dialog, on the **Twitter Widget** tab:

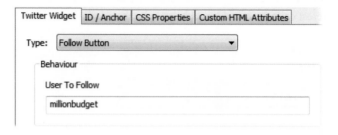

- From the **Type** drop-down list, select **Follow Button**.

- In the **User To Follow** input box, type your Twitter username.

- Click **OK**.

The Twitter Follow button is added to the page.

To add a Google +1 button:

1. On the **Quick Build** tab, in the **Social Media** category, click **Google +1 Button**.

2. Click once under the Twitter Follow button.

3. In the **Insert Google +1 Button** dialog, on the **Google +1 Button** tab:

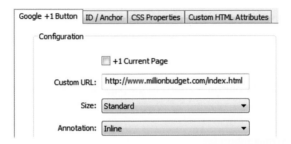

- Ensure the **+1 Current Page** option is not selected.

- In the **Custom URL** input box, type 'http://www.millionbudget.com/index.html'.

> The two settings above ensure the Home page is recommended on the visitor's Google+ network rather than the Support page.

- From the **Annotation** drop-down list, select **Inline**.

- Click **OK**.

The Google +1 button is added to the page.

To add a Facebook Like button:

1. On the **Quick Build** tab, in the **Social Media** category, click **Facebook Widget**.

2. Click once under the Google +1 button.

3. In the **Insert Facebook Widget** dialog, on the **Facebook Widget** tab:

  • From the **Type** drop-down list, select **Like Button**.

  • Click **OK**.

The Facebook Like button is added to the page under the Google +1 button.

Save your work by pressing **Ctrl+S**.

Feel free to **Preview** your changes. (See p. 7 for details.)

Bookmarking your site

In this final section, we'll explore how you can quickly add a range of social media buttons to your site to allow visitors to share your website with all their contacts. We'll add this to the Master page so it appears on all site pages.

To add a bookmarking button strip:

1. On the **Pages** tab, click **Master Pages**, and then double-click the **Master A** thumbnail.

2. On the **Quick Build** tab, in the **Social Media** category, click **Social Bookmarking Button Strip**.

3. Click anywhere on the page.

4. In the **Insert Social Bookmarking Button Strip** dialog, on the **Social Bookmarking Button Strip Configuration** tab:

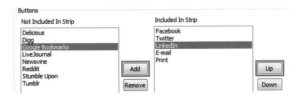

- From the **Not Included In Strip** list, select a social media platform and click **Add**.

- From the **Included In Strip** list, select an entry and click **Up** or **Down**, to reorder it in the list.

- Under the **Share** option, select **Page**. This will share, or bookmark, the current page rather than the site.

- From the **Target Window or Frame** section, from the drop-down list, select **New Window** and then click **OK**.

5. With the button strip still selected, drag the object's move button to position it neatly on the footer panel. (We placed it central.)

Feel free to **Preview** your changes. (See p. 7 for details.)

That's it! We have now explored some of the options for linking to various social media platforms. Feel free to experiment with the other widgets. See the *Social Media* book in WebPlus Help.

Save your work by pressing **Ctrl+S.**

Adding a search facility

 15 min

A search facility allows visitors to quickly find information on your website, particularly if it contains numerous pages or lots of text.

By the end of this tutorial you will be able to:

- Add new pages.

- Add a search results frame.

- Add a search input box.

If you have already completed the *Linking to social media* tutorial on p. 119, you can use your saved project as the starting point for this tutorial.

Let's begin...

* Open the **WPX8 Tutorial 07.wpp** project file (see p. 16 for details).

> ⬦ Alternatively, in the **Open** dialog, navigate to the folder where you saved your project file from the *Linking to social media* tutorial on p. 119, select it and click **Open**.

A partially designed site will open in the workspace.

Adding pages

First, we need to create a new blank page on which to display the results of the search. We'll exclude this page from site navigation so it only appears if the search facility is used.

To add blank pages:

I. On the **Pages** tab, click the down arrow on the ⊞ ▾ **Add new page or link** button and select **New Blank Page**.

2. In the **Page Properties** dialog:

* In the **Page name** input box, drag to select the default name and then type 'Search'.

* Select the **Specify page title** option and update the contents of the adjacent input box.

- In the **File name** input box, drag to select the default name and then type 'search.html'.

- In the **Navigation Options** section, from the **Navigation** drop-down list, select **Exclude page from site navigation**.

- In the **Placement** section, select **After** and then select **Sitemap** from the drop-down list.

3. Click **OK**.

The new page is added to the site and displayed in the workspace and on the Site tab.

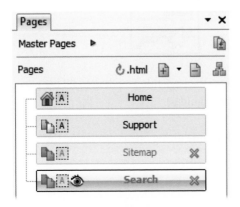

Now let's add our search facility.

Adding a search results frame

The search facility is built from two components—an input box where a visitor will type their search terms and a frame where the search results will display. These both need adding to your site. We'll start with the results frame.

To add a search results frame to the page:

1. On the **Quick Build** tab, in the **Smart Objects** category, click **Site Search Results Frame**.

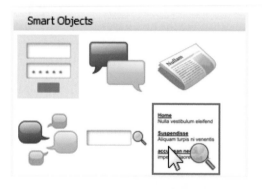

2. Position the cursor below the page title and drag to fill the page (using the blue margins as guides).

The **Insert Site Search Frame** dialog opens displaying the **Site Search Results Frame** tab.

3. In the **Results** section:

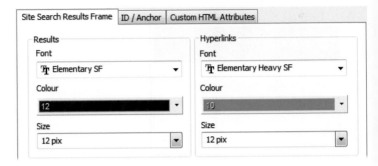

- From the **Font** drop-down list, select **Elementary SF**.

- From the **Colour** drop-down list, select **Scheme Colour 12**.

- From the **Size** drop-down list, select **12 pix**.

4. In the **Hyperlinks** section:

- From the **Font** drop-down list, select **Elementary Heavy SF**.

- From the **Colour** drop-down list, select **Scheme Colour 10**.

- From the **Size** drop-down list, select **12 pix**.

5. Click **OK**.

The search results frame is added to the page and populated with placeholder text.

Next, we'll add an input box for visitors to type their search terms.

 Save your work by pressing **Ctrl+S.**

Adding a search input box

We'll use the **Online Search** option for our search input box. This will enable a user's search terms to match with text content on pages in your site, as well as any Smart Objects (such as blogs and forums) placed on the page.

Online Search uses the Site Membership Manager facility created using Serif Web Resources. You'll need to create a Serif Web Resources account and then a Site Membership Manager if you wish to use the Online Search option.

To add a search input box to the site:

1. On the **Pages** tab, click **Master Pages**, and then double-click the **Master A** thumbnail.

2. On the **Quick Build** tab, in the **Smart Objects** category, click **Site Search Form**.

3. Click anywhere on the page.

4. In the **Insert Site Search Form** dialog:

- From the **Search Type** section, ensure the **Online Search** option is selected.

This option ensures that the search also includes words used in any Smart objects you have added to your site (or add in the future).

 If you do not intend on adding Smart objects to your site, you can use the **Client-side Search** which will search text added to your site within WebPlus only.

- From the **Smart Search Properties** section, click **Select Site Membership Manager**.

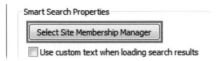

5. In the **Site Base URL** dialog:

- Type the web address (starting http://) of your website. E.g. http://www.millionbudget.com

- Click **OK**.

If you are not logged into Serif Web Resources, you'll be presented with the **Serif Web Resources Login** dialog.

Enter your **Username** and **Password** then click **Login**.

If you don't have a Serif Web Resources account, you can sign up by adding details to the **New User?** Section and clicking **Signup**.

6. In the **Site Membership Managers** dialog, click **Create New**.

7. In the **Configure** dialog:

- In the **Name** input box, type the name of the Site Membership Manager. We recommend giving this the same name as your WebPlus site name.

- In the **Site URL** input box, type the web address (starting http://) of your website.

- Click **Create**.

8. Back in the **Site Membership Managers** dialog, select your Site Membership Manager.

9. Back in the **Insert Site Search Form** dialog, click **OK**.

The search input box is added to the page.

10. With the input box still selected, drag the object's move button to position it neatly on the header panel. (We placed it bottom-right.)

That's it! We now have a search facility established on our site. When a visitor types words into the input box and clicks **Search**, the website will redirect them to the Search page and display the results there.

You now have a site which contains the essential components which will help visitors find the information they need when accessing your site. You can now publish this site online. Alternatively, you may wish to create a mobile-ready site from it. See the *Publishing your site* and *Making a mobile-ready site* tutorials starting on the following page and p. 153, respectively, for details.

Save your work by pressing **Ctrl+S.**

Publishing your site

 30 min

Once you have made your site, the next step is to publish it to the internet. We'll take you through the steps in this tutorial.

By the end of this tutorial you will be able to:

- Preview your site in WebPlus at different screen resolutions.

- Prepare your website for publication.

- Set up your FTP account.

- Publish and maintain your website.

> If you have already completed the *Adding a search facility* tutorial on p. 131, you can use your saved project as the starting point for this tutorial.

Let's begin...

* Open the **WPX8 Tutorial 08.wpp** project file (see p. 16 for details).

> Alternatively, in the **Open** dialog, navigate to the folder where you saved your project file from the *Adding a search facility* tutorial on p. 131, select it and click **Open**.

A completed site will open in the workspace.

Before we look at publishing the site to the web, let's first preview how the website will look.

Previewing your site

Previewing your site in a browser gives you a great indication of what the final published website will look like. We show you how to do this on p. 7. You can also preview your site directly in WebPlus, which allows you to view the site at different screen resolutions.

To preview your site in WebPlus:

1. On the **Standard** toolbar, click the arrow to expand the **Preview site** drop-down list.

2. Click the **Preview in Window (Internet Explorer)** option.

   WebPlus displays the site preview in a built-in Microsoft Internet Explorer window.

3. On the context toolbar, from the **Screen preview resolution** drop-down list, select a preview size.

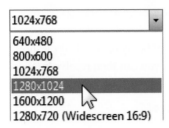

This allows you to determine how much of your page width is visible at certain resolutions.

4. When you've finished, click ⊗ **Close Preview**.

Preparing your website for publication

The **Task Monitor** tab displays a list of issues currently present in your site. It is worth running through these issues and resolving them before publishing your site online.

If you're using the supplied project file (WPX8 Tutorial 08.wpp), the following issues will be present:

- Form has no method of submission

- HTML text contains Lorem Ipsum

The numbers in parenthesis indicate how many times the issue occurs.

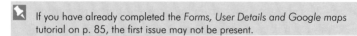 If you have already completed the *Forms, User Details and Google maps* tutorial on p. 85, the first issue may not be present.

If you're using other project files, you may have different or additional reported issues.

Each issue will have a unique way of being resolved. We'll show you the process of locating the issue so you can then resolve it.

To locate an issue to resolve:

• On the **Task Monitor** tab:

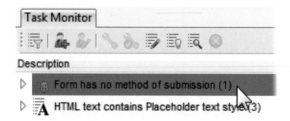

• Click to select the issue.

• Click 🔍 **Display Object**.

In the workspace the page object will be selected.

If the issue was **Form has no method of submission**, you can follow the Form submission via Serif Web Resources procedure in the *Forms, User Details and Google maps* tutorial on p. 85 to resolve the issue.

The **Task Monitor** tab also provides a **Program Hints** section which you may wish to work through before publishing your site.

For more information on using the **Task Monitor** tab and resolving issues, see *Task Monitor tab* in WebPlus Help.

When you are satisfied all issues with your website have been resolved (or you're happy to leave them unresolved), you can set up your FTP account and publish to the world wide web.

 Save your work by pressing **Ctrl+S.**

Setting up your FTP account

 You will only have to set up your FTP account the first time you publish your site to the web.

Now it's time to publish our site to a live location. Even though you may have saved your website as a WebPlus project, it's not truly a 'website' until you've converted it to files that can be viewed in a browser. WebPlus does this automatically when you publish the site.

 Useful terms to know:

• **FTP** - File Transfer Protocol—this is the standard way of uploading your website's files from your computer to your web host.

• **URL** - Universal Resource Locator—this is the 'address' where your website resides on the web.

• **Web Host** - this is a company which provides web space for you to store the files necessary to display your website pages on the internet.

 The next steps assume that you have dedicated space on a web server. If you are unsure how to access this, contact your Web host.

To set up your FTP account:

1. [icon] On the **Standard** toolbar, click the arrow to expand the **Publish site** drop-down list.

2. Click [icon] **Publish to Web**.

3. If the **Publish To Web: Get Hosting** dialog displays, click **Add Details**.

4. In the **Publishing Options** dialog, click **Manage Accounts**.

   The **Account Details** dialog will open.

5. When publishing to the Web you'll need to provide the following information, which you can obtain from your Web Host. (When you receive this information, usually displayed on-screen or sent by email on purchase of your web space, it is worth printing out for your own records and for later reference.)

- **Use SFTP:** This is a file transfer variant which some Web hosts use. Select the option if indicated to do so by your Web host.

- **Account name:** A descriptive name for this connection. This can be any name of your choice. You'll use it to identify this account in WebPlus (you may have more than one).

- **FTP address:** The URL that locates the internet-based server that will store your files—it will look similar to a Web address but often starts 'ftp.' or 'ftp://'. The FTP address is supplied by your Web host.

- **Port number:** Unless directed by your Web host, leave the **Port number** set at 21. This is the default port used by most FTP servers for file transfer.

- **Folder:** Allows you to upload sites to sub-folders of your main website's address. You can leave this blank unless you are directed otherwise by your Web host, or you want to publish to a specific sub-folder. (This may also be needed to correctly route your upload specifically to your own Web space.)

- **Username:** Specified by your Web host—this is often case-sensitive.

- **Password:** Specified by your Web host—this is often case-sensitive.

- **Passive Mode:** Leave checked (by default) unless you experience upload problems.

- **Website URL:** The web address of your site—it often starts 'http://' or 'https://'.

- Click **OK**.

> For more information about setting up your account details, see *Publishing to the web* in WebPlus Help.

Before you proceed further, it's a good idea to test your account settings to ensure there are no issues with connecting to the internet.

To test your account details and connection:

- In the **FTP Accounts** dialog, click **Test**.

  WebPlus will attempt to connect to your hosting account.

  You will be informed if the connection has been successful:

  - If unsuccessful, select your FTP Account from the **Account** drop-down list and click **Edit** to review your settings.

  - If successful, click **Update Account**—your new FTP account and settings are displayed in the **Publishing Options** dialog. (Your FTP account details are saved for future use.) Click **OK**.

Once you've set up your FTP account and can connect your computer to the host, publishing to the Web is simply a matter of transferring files.

Publishing to the web

With your FTP account set up and project ready-to-go, let's get onto the exciting task of getting your site onto the web!

 If you're currently in the main workspace, click **File>Publish Site>Publish to Web** to access the **Publish To Web** dialog.

To publish your site to the web:

1. In the **Publish to Web** dialog:

- Your current FTP account details should be displayed.

 If not, click **Change**, select an account from the **FTP account** drop-down list, and click **OK**.

- Any unresolved issues on your site are displayed in the **Tasks** section.

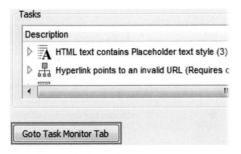

To resolve these issues before you publish your site, click **Goto Task Monitor Tab**. (This will cancel the publishing process.)

- Click **OK**.

  WebPlus will convert your design into HTML pages with
  associated graphics and other files, then begin to upload
  your site to the internet, showing individual file progress
  and overall progress.

2. When WebPlus has exported the selected pages, in the
Uploading files dialog, click **Close**.

3. To view your site online, in the **Web Site Publishing** dialog,
select a browser from the **in this browser** drop-down list and
click **View this URL**.

Your browser will launch showing the specified URL.

Now that your website is live on the web. Let's take a quick look at
how you update and maintain it.

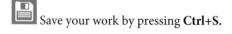 Save your work by pressing **Ctrl+S**.

Maintaining your website

The great thing about websites is the ability to update them
frequently at no extra cost—in fact, visitors will expect your website
to be up-to-date with all the latest information. With WebPlus, it's
quick to update a modified website which has been previously
published.

To update a previously published website:

1. With your WebPlus project still open in your workspace, make
   any necessary changes and then save your work.

2. From the **File** menu, click **Publish Site** and then select **Publish
   to Web**.

3. In the **Publish To Web** dialog:

- In the **Page Range** section, ensure the **Publish All Pages**
  option is not selected.

- Select the **Home** page option.

- Click **OK**.

4. In the **Uploading Files** dialog, select **Incremental Update** or **Full Upload**.

   - **Incremental Update:** WebPlus will export your site and compare the exported files to those already on the server. It will only upload files that are new or have changed since the last upload. This option can also check for missing files. Incremental updates are great when you want to quickly replace minor elements of your site!

   - **Full Upload:** WebPlus will upload all the files, regardless of whether they have changed since the last upload.

     In both cases you can instruct WebPlus to delete uploaded files that are no longer required by selecting this option in the dialog.

By only uploading pages which have changed (and selecting **Incremental Update**) you will notice that the web upload is much quicker. You can view your updated page in a browser.

 You can maintain your published website further by using the **Maintain Website** dialog (accessible from **File>Publish Site**). For more information, see *Maintaining your website* in WebPlus Help.

That's it! You've published your site to the Web for all to see! As you can see, WebPlus makes it very easy to publish your site and upload new content.

 If you're having problems we suggest you check your provider's website to find the information you need, or contact their customer support team.

Note: Serif cannot supply you with this information unless you have a Serif web hosting account.

Making a mobile-ready site

60 min

Websites designed for viewing on 'desktop' devices can be viewed using mobile devices. However, if you have the time, you may wish to consider creating a site which is designed specifically for viewing on mobile devices such as smart phones and tablets.

By the end of this tutorial you will be able to:

- Set up page redirects.

- Create a mobile site from a desktop site.

- Modify Master page design and objects.

- Preview your site at mobile screen resolution.

- Publish your mobile site to the web.

Let's begin...

- Open the **WPX8 Tutorial 08.wpp** project file (see p. 16 for details).

 Alternatively, in the **Open** dialog, navigate to the folder where you saved your project file from the *Adding a search facility* tutorial on p. 131, select it and click **Open**.

A completed site will open in the workspace.

WebPlus lets you create mobile solutions for your website in several ways:

- Create a **standalone mobile site**.

- Create a **hybrid desktop - mobile site**, with redirection from desktop pages to mobile site pages (and vice versa), all within the same WebPlus project.

  See *Creating mobile sites and pages* in WebPlus Help for more information.

- Create a **separate desktop and mobile site**, with redirect from desktop pages to a separately hosted mobile site. Your mobile site is created as a separate WebPlus project.

  We'll explore this option in this tutorial.

Setting up page redirects

Setting up page redirects is a quick and easy process in WebPlus. First, we'll show you how to redirect visitors from the main Home page to the mobile version, if they access the website from a mobile device.

To redirect to a mobile page:

1.  With the Home page displayed in the workspace, on the context toolbar, click **Page Properties**.

2. In the **Page Properties** dialog:

- On the left, select the **Redirect** category.

- Click **Link** next to the **Redirect to** box.

3. In the **Edit Page Redirect** dialog:

No Hyperlink	Internet Page	Creates a hyperlink to an internet page
Site Page	Hyperlink Information	
Internet Page	URL address: http://www.millionbudget.com/mobile/index.html	
Internet Email		

- Select the **Internet Page** category.

- In the **URL address** input box, type the web address of the Home page of the mobile site—http://www.millionbudget.com/mobile/index.html. (We will discuss this choice on p. 171.)

- Click **OK**.

4. Back in the **Page Properties** dialog, select **Redirect only on condition** option and then select **If recognised mobile device**.

5. Click **OK**.

Now, when a visitor accesses the Home page of the desktop site from a mobile device they will be immediately redirected to the Home page of the mobile site.

You may wish to follow the procedure above to set up a redirect from the **Support** page to **http://www.millionbudget.com/mobile/support.html** and the **Sitemap** page to **http://www.millionbudget.com/mobile/sitemap.html**. (There is no need to redirect the **Search** page, as it is only accessible via the search facility.)

 Save your work by pressing **Ctrl+S.**

Creating a mobile site from a previously created site

You can create a mobile site based on the pages created for your desktop site. First we'll save our project as a new, mobile project.

To save to a new project:

1. From the **File** menu, select **Save As**.

2. In the **Save As** dialog:

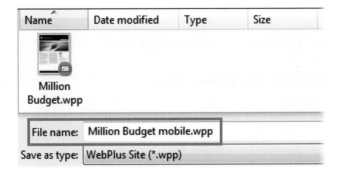

- In the **File name** input box, modify the current project name.

- Click **Save**.

Now you are working in a new project, any changes you make will not affect the desktop site.

Before we get stuck into the redesign of our site, we'll modify the redirects to ensure anyone accessing the mobile site pages on a desktop device will be redirected to the desktop site.

To redirect to a desktop page:

1. With the Home page displayed in the workspace, on the context toolbar, click **Page Properties**.

2. In the **Page Properties** dialog:

- On the left, select the **Redirect** category.

- Click **Link** next to the **Redirect to** box.

3. In the **Edit Page Redirect** dialog:

- In the **URL address** input box, type the web address of the Home page of the desktop site— http://www.millionbudget.com/index.html.

- Click **OK**.

4. Back in the **Page Properties** dialog:

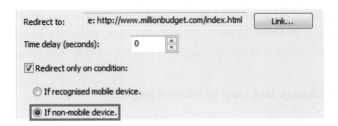

- Select the **If non-mobile device** option.

- Click **OK**.

Now, when a visitor accesses the Home page of the mobile site from a non-mobile device they will be immediately redirected to the Home page of the desktop site.

You may wish to follow the procedure above to set up a redirect from the **Support** page to **http://www.millionbudget.com/support.html** and the **Sitemap** page to **http://www.millionbudget.com/sitemap.html**.

 Save your work by pressing **Ctrl+S.**

Creating mobile-sized pages

One major difference between non-mobile and mobile devices is the width of the screen. So the first step in adapting the design of a site is to modify the width of the site's pages. We'll do this using the **Site Manager**.

To change the size of all site pages:

1. On the context toolbar, select 📷 **Site Manager**.

2. In the **Site Manager** dialog:

   • On the left, select the **Page Properties** category.

   • Select the check box on the **Page** column to select all the listed pages.

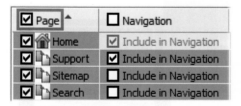

   • At the bottom of the **Width (pix)** column, set the width to **320**.

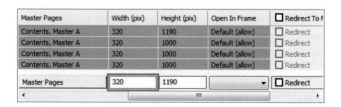

This will set the width of all selected pages to 320 pix.

- (Optional) At the bottom of the **Height (pix)** column, set the height to **2090**.

- On the left, select the **Master Page Properties** category.

- Click in the **Width (pix)** column and set the width to **320**.

- Click **Close**.

The Master page and all other page sizes update to fit our new settings.

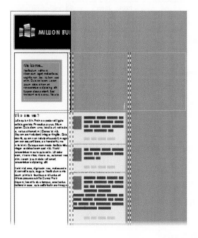

The content looks disorganized, but we'll correct this next.

You may wish to update the default size of new pages added to the site to match the current page size. From the Properties menu, select Site Properties, and then adjust the settings from the Page Size sub-category (Page category).

Setting up margins

Before we begin reorganizing our design, we'll set up margins to work against.

To set up margins:

1. On the context toolbar, click ▦ **Site Properties**.

2. In the **Site Properties** dialog:

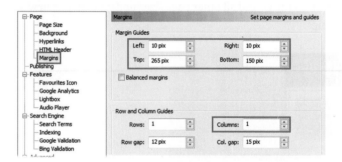

- On the left, from the **Page** category, select the **Margins** sub-category.

- Set the **Left** and **Right** margins to **10 pix**.

- Set the **Top** margin to **265 pix**.

- Set the **Bottom** margin to **150 pix**.

- In the **Row and Column Guides** section, set the **Columns** to **1**.

- Click **OK**.

The above settings will ensure margin guides appear consistently on all pages, regardless of their width or height. We can now rework our page content to fit with these margins.

 Save your work by pressing **Ctrl+S**.

Reworking Master page content

Our content reorganization will begin on the Master page before moving onto individual site pages. We'll not step through every procedure, but will discuss the major issues you will need to address.

To rework the header:

1. On the **Pages** tab, click **Master Pages**, and then double-click the **Master A** thumbnail.

2. 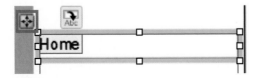 Select the Frame text Page name object and drag the object's move button to position it neatly within the page margins.

3. Drag each header object to the pasteboard until you are left with just the panel partially on the page.

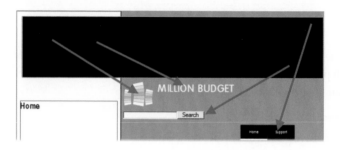

4. Select the panel and then, on the **Transform** tab:

- Ensure the object is set to **Anchor Top Left** and the **Aspect Ratio** is **Unlocked**.

- Set **X** to **10 pix** and **Y** to **10 pix**.

- Set **W** (Width) to **300 pix** and **H** (Height) to **245 pix**.

  The panel is resized and positioned on the page precisely.

5. Reposition the header objects on the header as desired.

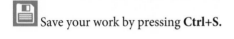
You may have to resize the navigation bar to fit the new header size.

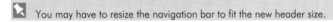 Save your work by pressing **Ctrl+S.**

The navigation bar will probably look better centred like the other header elements.

To change navigation bar alignment:

1. Double-click the navigation bar on the page.

2. In the **Edit Navigation Bar** dialog, select the **Appearance** tab.

3. From the categories on the left, select **Layout**.

4. From the **Horizontal Alignment** drop-down list, select **Centre**.

5. Click **OK**.

The navigation bar updates on the page.

You can apply the above procedures to the rework the Master page footer. We used the Transform tab again to resize and position the panel...

To resize and position the footer panel:

1. Select the panel and then, on the **Transform** tab:

- Ensure the object is set to **Anchor Top Left** and the **Aspect Ratio** is **Unlocked**.

- Set **W** (Width) to **300 pix** and **H** (Height) to **130 pix**.

2. Drag the panel's ⊕ move button to position it neatly in the centre of the page, below the bottom margin.

...and then repositioned the footer objects.

It is unlikely a visitor would print the web page from a mobile device, so we'll remove this option from the Social Bookmarking Button Strip.

To modify a bookmarking button strip:

1. Double-click the **Social Bookmarking Button Strip** on the page.

2. In the **Edit Social Bookmarking Button Strip** dialog, on the **Social Bookmarking Button Strip Configuration** tab:

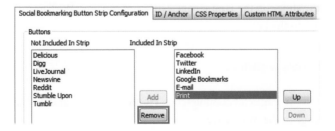

- From the **Included In Strip** list, select **Print** and click **Remove**.

- Click **OK**.

The Social Bookmarking Button Strip updates on the page.

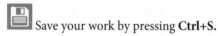 Save your work by pressing **Ctrl+S.**

Reworking page content

During the design of our desktop site we restricted many of the page objects to 300 pix wide. This makes it extremely easy to rework the page content for our mobile site. With most objects, simply reposition them within the page margins!

Other page objects, such as the Google map on the Support page and the slider on the Home page, will need resizing. We'll examine how to do the latter.

To resize a slider:

1. On the **Pages** tab, double-click **Home** to select it and display the page in the workspace.

2. Click to select the slider.

3. On the object's toolbar, click ▶ **Show Next Panel**.

4. Click to select the picture on the slider panel.

5. On the **Transform** tab, set the **W** (Width) to **300 pix**.

6. On the object toolbar, click  **Position Image**, and drag on the picture to position it better.

7. With the picture still select, on the object's toolbar, click **Select Parent** to select the slider.

8. Repeat steps 3-6 for the second image.

9. Click to select the slider and, on the **Transform** tab, set the **W** (Width) to **300 pix**.

> Alternatively, you can edit your slider in Slider Studio. See the *Sliders and text* tutorial on p. 63 for more information.

Your slider and its content will now be resized neatly for the page.

Save your work by pressing **Ctrl+S.**

Previewing your site

Previewing your site in WebPlus gives you a great indication of what the final published website will look like on a mobile device.

To preview your site in WebPlus:

1. On the **Standard** toolbar, click the arrow to expand the **Preview site** drop-down list, and then:

   - Select **Disable Page Redirects when Previewing**.

     This will allow you to preview the mobile site despite working on a desktop computer.

   - Click the **Preview in Window (Internet Explorer)** option.

     WebPlus displays the site preview in a built-in Microsoft Internet Explorer window.

2. On the context toolbar, from the **Screen preview resolution** drop-down list, select **320x480 (iPhone 3G)**.

3. When you have finished previewing your site, click **Close Preview**.

Once you're happy with your mobile site design, it's time to publish it!

Publishing to the web

> The procedure below assumes you have already published your desktop site
> to the web. If you have not done this yet, we highly recommend you
> complete the *Publishing your site* tutorial on p. 141 before proceeding.

At the beginning of this tutorial we set up a redirect from our desktop
site to our mobile site (see p. 155). We redirected our Home page to
the URL 'http://www.millionbudget.com/mobile/index.html'. Look
carefully and you will see **mobile/** in the middle. This indicates that
our mobile site should be published to a sub-folder (named 'mobile')
on our web space to make it accessible.

We'll show you how to do this.

To set up a mobile-specific FTP account:

1. From the **File** menu, click **Publish Site** and then, select **Publish
to Web**.

2. In the **Publish To Web** dialog, click **Change**.

3. In the **Publishing Options** dialog, click **Manage Accounts**.

4. In the **FTP Accounts** dialog:

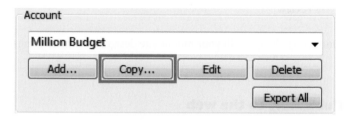

- From the **Account** drop-down list, select the account you used to upload the desktop version of the website.

- Click **Copy**.

5. In the **Account Details** dialog:

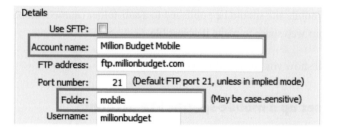

- In the **Account name** input box, add 'Mobile' to the account name. For example, Million Budget Mobile.

- In the **Folder** input box, type 'mobile'.

- Click **OK**.

6. Back in the **FTP Accounts** dialog, click **Update Account**.

7. Back in the **Publishing Options** dialog, click **OK**.

The **Publishing to** details in the **Publish To Web** dialog have now updated. Now you are ready to upload your mobile-ready site!

To publish your site to the web:

1. In the **Publish to Web** dialog:

- Any unresolved issues on your site are displayed in the **Tasks** section.

  To resolve these issues before you publish your site, click **Goto Task Monitor Tab**. (This will cancel the publishing process.)

  See the *Preparing your website for publication* procedure in the *Publishing your site* tutorial on p. 143 for more information.

- Click **OK**.

  WebPlus will convert your design into HTML pages with associated graphics and other files.

2. In the **FTP Error** dialog, click **Create Directory**.

WebPlus will begin to upload your site to the internet, showing individual file progress and overall progress.

3. When WebPlus has exported the selected pages, in the **Uploading files** dialog, click **Close**.

4. In the **Web Site Publishing** dialog, click **Close**. To view your mobile site online, you will need to use a mobile device.

5. Simply type your website address (e.g. millionbudget.com) in the browser on your mobile device and you'll see the mobile version of your Home page display!

That's it! You now have a mobile-ready site for visitors to access via their portable devices.

 Save your work by pressing **Ctrl+S.**

Creative
Showcase

2

Pro Templates

WebPlus provides a selection of **Pro Template** sites that are populated with pictures and text placeholders which you can start using straight away.

To open a Pro Template site:

1. On the **File** menu, click **Startup Assistant**.

2. On the left, click **Templates**.

3. On the **Templates** list, select **WebPlus X8 Pro Templates**, and from the thumbnail gallery, click to select a site from one of the templates.

4. Click **OK**.

We'll showcase the **Ready Digital Marketing** (as selected above), **Stack & Stone** and **Ski Resort & Leisure** templates next.

 You can get more **Pro Template Packs** from Serif's template store. Visit http://www.serif.com/templates

Ready Digital Marketing

Stack & Stone

Ski Resort & Leisure

Theme Layouts

WebPlus provides a selection of **Theme Layout** templates with picture and text placeholders that you can use as starting points for your own sites.

To open a theme layout site:

1. On the **File** menu, click **Startup Assistant**.

2. On the left, click **Templates**.

3. On the **Templates** list, select **Theme Layouts**, and from the thumbnail gallery, click to select a site from one of the Theme Layout templates.

Kitsch   Ledger   Level

4. Click **OK**.

We'll showcase the **Level** (as selected above), **Partition**, and **Ecrue** templates next. We have added a picture to the placeholder picture frames for clarity.

Level

Partition

Ecrue